ISSUES THAT CONCERN YOU

Gangs

Other books in the Issues That Concern You series:

Gangs

Peggy Daniels, *Book Editor*

Christine Nasso, *Publisher*
Elizabeth Des Chenes, *Managing Editor*

GREENHAVEN PRESS

An imprint of Thomson Gale, a part of The Thomson Corporation

Detroit • New York • San Francisco • New Haven, Conn. • Waterville, Maine • London

LIBRARY OF CONGRESS CATALOGING-IN-PUBLICATION DATA

Gangs / Peggy Daniels, book editor.
    p. cm. -- (Issues that concern you)
  Includes bibliographical references and index.
  ISBN 978-0-7377-3815-5 (hardcover)
  1. Gangs--United States. I. Daniels, Peggy.
  HV6439.U5G3585 2008
  364.1'0660973--dc22

2007032861

Printed in the United States of America

10 9 8 7 6 5 4 3 2 1

CONTENTS

As computers and the Internet become more common in the lives of young people across the United States, more and more gangs are also using this technology. Many gangs have their own Web sites featuring graffiti images, gang symbols, and photographs of members displaying hand signs, weapons, drugs, and money. Pages on popular social networking sites allow gangs to expand their presence online, reaching and recruiting more young people than ever before. Videos of gang initiations and criminal activities are often posted to brag or intimidate enemies.

Gang activity online—known as "netbanging" or "web banging"—glorifies the gang lifestyle and culture and encourages face-to-face violence in the real world. Gang members use the Web to communicate with each other in discussion forums, bulletin boards, and online chat rooms. Often using coded language or slang to discuss plans for future crimes or initiations, gangs can coordinate activities and issue orders on the Web. For example, police departments throughout the United States have found that fights between rival gangs were scheduled online, with the locations and times of the brawls posted ahead of time.

All of this information is available to savvy Web users who know how to use an Internet search engine—including many curious children and teens. And even if Internet users are not looking specifically for gangs online, simple Web surfing can lead young people to sites that promote gang violence and crime. Most social networking sites have policies against illegal content and work to immediately remove words, pictures, and videos featuring violence and illegal acts. But with an estimated 1 billion people using the Internet worldwide, it is extremely difficult to monitor and control gangs who are intent on advertising themselves online. For every gang member who is banned from posting on a networking or community site, there are many more that are ready and able to take their place online.

Organized Gangs Online

According to the 2005 National Gang Threat Assessment report of the National Alliance of Gang Investigators' Associations (www .nagia.org/), gangs are also using technology to commit more serious crimes. Wireless Internet connections and computer databases are being used to coordinate larger criminal enterprises such as national or international drug sales. Advanced gang organizations use computers to create fake bank checks and counterfeit money. Gangs also use the Internet to sell pornography and operate prostitution rings and illegal gambling sites. And sales of illegally copied software, music, and movies are increasing among online gangs.

Family members of people killed by gang violence mourn while visiting the 3rd Annual Victim's Rights Vigil in Los Angeles.

Many police departments report that these online activities often result in physical violence among rival gangs.

Some gangs are expanding their illegal activities to include identity theft, using Internet and e-mail scams or computer viruses to steal personal information such as credit card account numbers or online banking passwords. Theft and fraud schemes are expected to increase as gang members become more skilled in their use of the Internet. Other sophisticated gangs use the Internet to track legal prosecutions and court proceedings brought against gang members. By accessing publicly available government information online, gangs attempt to identify prosecuting attorneys, judges, and witnesses as targets for intimidation. Gangs are expected to continue using advanced technology as their expanding presence online attracts more technically skilled members.

Youth at Risk

A 2006 survey conducted by the Pew Internet & American Life Project (www.pewinternet.org/) found that an estimated 87 percent of young people aged twelve to seventeen are Internet users. Nearly half of all gang members also fall into this age group. The overlap of active Internet users and potential gang members based on age indicates that gang member wannabes can easily come into contact with gangs online. Isolated young people can learn about gang clothing, colors, and hand signs from Web sites and postings intended to make gangs seem cool. Adolescents and teens who want to fit in, belong to a group, or "be somebody" may imitate the gang members they see online, placing themselves and others in danger.

Although most gangs only accept members from their own neighborhood or community, some larger, international gangs are beginning to recruit new members in different cities. Gang-related Web sites present dangerous opportunities for young people to become caught up in activities that are much more serious than they may have imagined. Gang members and wannabes often believe that the gang offers many benefits such as money, power, protection, and safety; however, these false perceptions ignore the harsh realities of gang association. Membership in a gang has severe consequences, most notably that gang members are sixty times more likely to be killed than are nonmembers. Young people creating, visiting, or participating in gang-related Web sites are placing themselves at risk of being mistaken for gang members by police and of becoming involved in dangerous illegal activities.

Policing Gangs Online

With the rise of Internet-based gang activity, the Web has become a valuable antigang resource for police departments across the country. Police officers patrol a new, virtual beat by visiting and monitoring gang-related Web sites, often on a daily basis. Gang Web sites, online postings, and transcripts of Internet chat rooms can be important supplements to traditional police work. Information posted online by gang members can be used to investigate crimes, track down suspects, and inform and educate the public about community gang problems. Images of gang-related hand signs, graffiti symbols, tattoos, colors, and clothing are used by police officers and concerned community members to identify gang members. Boasts about gang operations and warnings to rival gangs to stay away from certain gang territories also help police know where to find gang members. In some cases, information posted online has resulted in gang members being arrested and put in jail. In this way, gang members who brag online about their status or the crimes they have committed are actually helping police officers to crack down on local gang activity.

With gangs present in so many communities and schools this issue clearly affects all teens. In *Issues That Concern You: Gangs*, the authors debate the effectiveness and fairness of such policies in excerpts from articles, books, reports, and other sources. In addition, the volume also includes resources for further investigation. The Organizations to Contact section gives students direct access to organizations that are leading the fight against gangs. The bibliography highlights recent books and periodicals for more in-depth study, while the appendix "What You Should Know About Gangs" outlines basic facts about gangs. Finally, the "What You Should

Do About Gangs" section helps students use their knowledge to help themselves and others. Taken together, these features make *Issues That Concern You: Gangs* a valuable resource for anyone researching this issue.

ONE

Gangs Are
a Serious Problem

Edward Cohn

Criminal gangs have been operating in the U.S. for many years, and are still a serious problem for communities across the country, contends Edward Cohn in the following viewpoint. Once limited primarily to cities and larger towns, street gangs have begun to establish themselves in rural areas, and imprisoned gang members are able to continue participating in criminal gang activities, Cohn asserts. Gangs threaten the security of U.S. citizens, the author maintains. Edward Cohn is executive director of the National Major Gang Task Force, which promotes partnership among law enforcement, criminal corrections, military agencies, and educational institutions to minimize the threats posed by gangs and other security-threatening groups.

The phenomenon of the gang culture continues to grow in numbers as well as in sophistication. Those who work in the criminal justice system and encounter the culture on a daily basis are very aware of the negative results gang activity has on all aspects of the community. However, most citizens, unless they are personally affected, have no idea or understanding of gang logistics. The sad commentary is that most citizens do not care

Edward Cohn, "The Gang Culture Continues to Grow," *Corrections Today*, vol. 68, April 2006, p. 6. Copyright © 2006 American Correctional Association, Inc. Reproduced by permission.

or refuse to acknowledge that there is a problem. In a recent survey of law enforcement agencies, 31 percent of the respondents indicated that their communities refused to acknowledge a gang problem.

Summary of U.S. Gang Activity Reports

Annual Maximum Number of Gangs, 2002–2004

Number of Gangs	Larger Cities	Suburban Counties	Smaller Cities	Rural Counties
No Data Reported	3.6%	12.0%	8.7%	4.0%
3 or Fewer	15.4%	24.7%	51.0%	58.6%
4–6	21.5%	20.4%	24.8%	22.2%
7–15	29.6%	22.6%	12.1%	11.1%
16–30	13.6%	7.1%	3.4%	4.0%
More than 30	16.4%	13.3%	0.0%	0.0%

Annual Maximum Number of Gang Members, 2002–2004

Number of Gang Members	Larger Cities	Suburban Counties	Smaller Cities	Rural Counties
No Data Reported	13.0%	31.5%	22.3%	19.2%
50 or Fewer	18.5%	27.2%	54.4%	60.6%
51–200	25.4%	17.7%	14.6%	18.2%
201–500	14.5%	9.2%	8.8%	2.0%
501–1,000	11.7%	4.6%	0.0%	0.0%
More than 1,000	16.9%	9.8%	0.0%	0.0%

Taken from: *National Youth Gang Survey Analysis*, National Youth Gang Center.

Lt. Bobby Shirley of the Jefferson County sheriff's department examines gang graffiti in rural West Virginia. Gangs are present throughout the United States.

A majority of people believe that gangs are located only in lower socioeconomic neighborhoods of major metropolitan areas. That is not true today. Migration is apparent as gangs that were once exclusive on the east and west coasts have found their way to other geographical areas of the country. Gangs that were exclusive in the urban areas now have worked their way into middle income neighborhoods and even into affluent neighborhoods. There is hardly an entity in our country that is not affected by gang activity.

History of Gangs

What is being experienced today commenced in the 1980s, when illegal gang activity was recognized in a few large metropolitan areas, including Chicago, Detroit and Los Angeles. However, by the end of the decade, the Blood and Crip Nations from Los Angeles and the People and Folk Nations from Chicago were moving and creating representation in metropolitan communities across America. And gangs have become even more widespread as they move to rural areas to set up business.

Organized gangs are not new. They have been around for centuries. The earliest recording of a gang is that of rebellious children mentioned in 2 Kings 2:23–25 of the Bible. From the late 1800s to the 1960s, neighborhood gangs included fighting and thrill seeking for youths. The Roaring '20s showed an increase in adult gangs, when they were highly organized and identified with the Prohibition Era. The evolution of gangs involved in criminal activities has continued to be motivated by money.

In the 1960s, the membership numbers of African American, Puerto Rican and Mexican American gangs rose to an all-time high. With membership increasing, levels of violence escalated as well. Having easy access to weapons and firearms made lethal violence the norm.

Gangs in Prisons and Communities

The numbers of gangs and gang members existing in the streets today are countless. Although there is no commonly recognized total figure [for gang activity inside prisons], in 2002 the National Major Gang Task Force published the findings of a survey completed by the College of Justice and Safety Center at Eastern Kentucky University. This study, "A Study of Gangs and Security Threat Groups in America's Adult Prisons and Jails," noted that the number of validated gangs existing in our institutions was 1,625. A 1985 survey by George and Camille Camp of Criminal Justice Institute listed a total of 140. In less than 20 years, the increase of gang members among the incarcerated population was very significant and can only leave to one's imagination the numbers actively preying upon our communities.

Are street gangs and incarcerated gangs related? Of course they are. Constant communication exists between street and incarcerated gang members. Incarceration often does little to disrupt activities. Leadership usually is able to exert influence on the street from within the prison. Phone calls, letters, visitation and assistance from corrupt staff enable them to carry on business as usual within the confines of prison. . . .

Gangs Are a Serious Problem

Before September 11, 2001, through appropriated funding and grants, agencies designed to monitor the existence of gangs and gang activity were able to share with each other surveillance and apprehension data. Since then, funding has not been readily made available, and many resources previously used in this area have been eliminated. For a period of time, little or no emphasis was placed on street gangs. One has to be concerned with the security of our nation's borders, infrastructure, transportation systems and citizens. However, there must be concern about what is going on in the streets of America's cities. There is no formal systematic approach to agencies dealing with this phenomenon. The sharing of information by related agencies and the citizens of each community is imperative if we are to achieve control over this nemesis. Leadership, whether elected or appointed, must not hide from reality and deny having a problem in their area of responsibility. It is a naive leader who believes he or she can ignore or deny an issue without consequences. We must be vigilant about the decay from within as well as potential destruction from the perimeter.

TWO

Gangs Affect Every Part of a Community

James C. Howell

> Gangs have a pervasive impact on the communities in which they operate, according to the author of the following viewpoint. Gang members have extensive involvement in various criminal activities that create fear and place public safety at risk, he contends. The impact of gang-related crime and violence disrupts every aspect of a community's ability to function normally, and gangs interfere with the operation of schools and businesses, cause increased economic stress, and restrict the freedom and independence of community members, the author maintains.
>
> James C. Howell has been affiliated with the U.S. Department of Justice for more than twenty-one years. He is a former director of the U.S. Office of Juvenile Justice and Delinquency Prevention and currently serves as a senior research associate at the National Youth Gang Center. He is the author of more than seventy publications, including the book *Juvenile Justice and Youth Violence*.

Although a major concern of residents is the more organized and violent gangs, the start-up gangs also instill fear in residents when troublesome behaviors involve intimidation, vandalism, graffiti, and occasional drug sales. Nevertheless, community residents'

James C. Howell, "The Impact of Gangs on Communities," *National Youth Gang Center Bulletin*, Tallahassee, FL, 2006. Reproduced by permission.

fear of gangs and of becoming victims of gang crime is very great in the most gang-infested communities. A study in Orange County, California, in which a random sample of residents were interviewed, illustrates this case. Fear of crime and gangs was an "immediate," daily experience for people who lived in lower-income neighborhoods where gangs were more prevalent and dangerous. But for people in other areas, fear was generally an abstract concern about the future that became immediate only when they entered certain pockets of the county. In the most gang-ridden areas, many residents reported having avoided gang areas because they were afraid of gangs and criminal victimization. Others talked about avoiding certain streets and taking a circuitous route to shopping areas at night to avoid gangs that operate in certain neighborhoods. Intimidation of other youths, adults, and business owners is not uncommon, and intimidation of witnesses or potential witnesses is particularly serious because it undermines the justice process.

In a few large cities, youth gangs and drug gangs have virtually taken over some public-housing developments. [A 1996 report] described one of the worst cases of gang dominance in Chicago's Robert Taylor Homes, a low-income public-housing development. In the early 1990s, gangs in the housing development were transformed from turf gangs to drug gangs, and an escalation of gang violence resulted. Use of zip guns and hand-to-hand fighting of the past had given way to powerful handguns, drive-by shootings, and some use of assault weapons. The personal safety of the residents themselves was jeopardized to the extent that the risk of being caught in gang cross fire was imminent. Other drug gangs operating as organized criminal groups have had devastating community impacts. New York City's Puerto Rican Black Park Gang, so named because it shot out lights surrounding its base of operations in a park to avoid police detection is a classic example. It was a very violent drug gang—believed to be responsible for 15 murders—that trafficked in drugs and used the proceeds to buy legitimate businesses through which it laundered drug profits. In addition to drug trafficking and violent crimes, the gang was involved in trafficking or using illegally obtained firearms and using force to intimidate witnesses and victims.

Gangs and Violent Crime

Of course, homicide is the crime of greatest concern to everyone. Reports of gang-related homicides are concentrated mostly in the largest cities in the United States, where there are long-standing and persistent gang problems and a greater number of documented gang members—most of whom are identified by law enforcement as young adults. In the 2002 and 2003 National Youth Gang Surveys [NYGS], nearly 4 out of 10 very large cities reported 10 or more gang homicides. However, the majority reported none or not more than one homicide.

Level of Gang Involvement in Crime (by type of crime)			
Level of Gang Involvement	**High (%)**	**Moderate (%)**	**Low (%)**	**None/ Unknown (%)**
Firearms Possession	23.5	13.7	19.6	43.2
Vandalism and Graffiti	23.5	25.5	13.7	37.3
Felonious Assault	21.6	21.6	21.6	35.2
Homicide	15.7	11.8	21.6	51.0
Burglary	9.8	21.6	19.6	49.0
Firearms Trafficking	9.8	19.6	17.6	52.9
Auto Theft	7.8	23.5	27.5	41.1
Intimidation and Extortion	5.9	15.7	31.4	44.0
Firearms Burglary	5.9	13.7	19.6	60.8

Taken from: *2005 National Gang Threat Assessment*, National Alliance of Gang Investigators Associations

Youth gangs are responsible for a disproportionate number of homicides. In two cities, Los Angeles and Chicago—arguably the most gang-populated cities in the United States—over half of the combined nearly 1,000 homicides reported in 2004 were attributed to gangs. Of the remaining 171 cities, approximately one-fourth of all the homicides were considered gang-related. More than 80% of gang-problem agencies, in both smaller cities and rural counties, recorded zero gang homicides. Across the United States, the number of gang homicides reported by cities with populations of 100,000 or more increased 34% from 1999 to 2003.

Jurisdictions experiencing higher levels of gang violence—evidenced by reports of multiple gang-related homicides over survey years—were significantly more likely than those experiencing no gang homicides to report that firearms were "used often" by gang members in assault crimes (47% versus 4% of the jurisdictions, respectively). Areas with longer-standing gang problems and a larger number of identified gang members—most often those with more adult-aged gang members—were also more likely to report greater firearm use by gang members in assault crimes.

Although the question of the extent to which street gangs shifted toward entrepreneurial activity in the 1980s and 1990s and the consequences of this shift are constantly debated by researchers, the reality is that gangs are often extensively involved in criminal activity. Although the proportion of all crimes committed by gang members is unknown, analyses of reported violent crimes in several cities reveal that their members often represent a large proportion of the high-rate violent offenders. Lethal violence related to gangs tends to be concentrated in the largest cities, which are mired with larger and ongoing gang problems. Frequent firearm use in assault crimes is typically reported in these larger cities.

Types of Gang Crime

Gang crime, however, resembles far more of a criminal smorgasbord than a main course of violence. National Youth Gang Survey respondents estimated the proportion of gang members who engaged in the following six serious and/or violent offenses in 2001: aggravated assault, robbery, burglary, motor vehicle theft, larceny/theft, and drug sales. Two clear patterns were seen. First, a large majority of agencies noted some gang member involvement in all six of the measured crimes. Second, the most frequent response was that none of these crimes were committed by a large proportion ("Most/All") of gang members within the jurisdiction, indicating considerable variability among gang members in terms of offending. Agencies that said a large proportion of gang members were involved in one or more of these offenses most often reported drug sales. A clear majority of law enforcement agencies in the NYGS report that while gang and drug problems overlap, it is typically only a subset of gang members in their jurisdiction who are actively involved in drug sales. These findings correspond with other research which finds an extensive amount of variation in the types of crimes in which gangs are involved. One noted gang researcher refers to this consistently uncovered pattern as "cafeteria-style" offending. . . .

Impact of Prison Gangs

The life cycle of many arrested gang members involves moving from communities to detention, to juvenile corrections, to adult prisons, and back into communities. The correctional system stage is but one segment of many gang members' "street life cycle."

It is widely recognized that national prison data seriously underestimates the proportion of all inmates that are gang-involved. However, in recent years, the issue of gang members returning from a secure confinement has received greater attention, in part, because of the growing numbers of inmates that are now released annually. A recent estimate is that nearly 600,000 adult inmates arrive on the doorsteps of communities throughout the country each year. More people are leaving prison today than at any time in history, and many lack preparation for life on the outside.

Recent NYGS findings reveal that returning members are a noticeable problem for approximately two-thirds of the gang-problem jurisdictions. Of the agencies reporting the return of gang members from confinement in 2001, nearly two-thirds (63%)

Ten-year-old Faheem Thomas-Childs was caught in the cross-fire of a gang battle outside his Philadelphia school and killed in 2004.

reported returning members "somewhat" or "very much" contributed to an increase in violent crime among local gangs; 69% reported the same for drug trafficking. Respondents said returning members had less of an impact on local gang activities, such as property crimes and weapons procurement; 10% or less reported returning members influenced each of these areas "very much." According to these respondents, the effect of returning members was typically observed in increases in violent crime and drug trafficking among local gangs. . . .

Gang members were more likely than nonmembers to be arrested, were rearrested more quickly following release from prison, were rearrested more frequently, and were more likely to be arrested for violent and drug offenses than were nongang members.

Impact of Immigration and Migration

The impact of gang migration on local gang problems is not as large as commonly perceived. First, there is very little evidence supporting the notion that youth gangs have the capacity to set up satellite operations in distant cities. Second, "gang migration" almost exclusively involves relocation of gang members with their families. The 2004 NYGS asked law enforcement respondents about gang member migration or the movement of actively involved gang youth from other jurisdictions. An analysis of survey results showed that a small number of agencies (10%) reported that more than half of the documented gang members in their jurisdiction had migrated from other areas, while a majority (60%) of respondents reported none or few (less than 25%) gang-member migrants. Among agencies experiencing a higher percentage of gang-member migration, 45% reported that social reasons (e.g., members moving with families or in pursuit of legitimate employment opportunities) affected local migration patterns "very much." Also reported, but to a lesser degree, were drug market opportunities (23%), avoidance of law enforcement crackdowns (21%), and participation in other illegal ventures (18%). Social reasons were significantly more likely to be reported among agencies experiencing higher levels of gang-member migration.

As a contributing factor to local gang problems, immigration may well be a more important factor than migration of gang members across our country. Heavy immigration, particularly from Latin America and Asia, has introduced extremely violent gangs, such as Mara Salvatrucha, to the United States. [A 2005 report] suggests that two California-based groups have drawn on the ebb and flow of migrants to become substantial threats to public safety: the 18th Street and Mara Salvatrucha 13 (MS-13) gangs. The MS-13 identify themselves with tattoos, such as the number 13, meaning "trece" in Spanish, shown as MS-13. The MS-13 gang is said to be involved in a variety of criminal enterprises, and they show no fear of law enforcement. They seem willing to commit almost any crime, and MS-13 gang members tend to have a higher level of criminal involvement than other gang members. . . . MS-13 members have been involved in burglaries, auto thefts, narcotic sales, home invasion robberies, weapons smuggling, carjacking, extortion, murder, rape, witness intimidation, illegal firearm sales, car theft, aggravated assaults, and drug trafficking. They also have been known to place a "tax" on prostitutes and non-gang member drug dealers who are working in MS-13 "turf." Failure to pay up will most likely result in violence. . . . MS-13 gang members are involved in exporting stolen U.S. cars to South America. The cars are often traded for contraband when dealing with drug cartels. . . . [Eighty percent] of the cars on El Salvador streets were stolen in the United States. Car theft is a lucrative business for the MS-13.

The Cost of Gang Violence

An informed estimate of the economic cost of gang crimes cannot be made because gang crimes are not routinely and systematically recorded in most law enforcement agencies. Hence, the proportion of all crimes attributable to gangs is unknown. In addition, the medical and financial consequences of gang violence, per se, are often overlooked. The total volume of crime is estimated to cost Americans $655 billion each year, and gangs are responsible for a substantial proportion of this. Gangs in the United States have long had a significant economic crime impact. A study of admissions to a Los Angeles hospital trauma center found that the costs of 272 gang-related gunshot victims totaled nearly $5 million (emergency room, surgical procedures, intensive care, and surgical ward stay), which equated to $5,550 per patient per day. More than a decade ago, the total medical cost of gang violence in Los Angeles County alone was estimated to exceed $1 billion annually. Nationwide, the complete costs of gun violence indicate a value of approximately $1 million per assault-related gunshot injury. A single adolescent criminal career of about ten years can cost taxpayers between $1.7 and $2.3 million.

Some gangs have become entrepreneurial organizations. Although it is rare, some gangs, such as the Black Gangster Disciples Nation, have evolved into formal adult criminal organizations. This gang is reputed to manage an extensive drug operation, perhaps involving tens of thousands of members in a number of states. Its corporate hierarchy consists of a chairman of the board, two boards of directors (one for prisons, another for the streets), governors (who control drug trafficking within geographical areas), regents (who supply the drugs and oversee several drug-selling locations within the governors' realm), area coordinators (who collect revenues from drug-selling spots), enforcers (who beat or kill members who cheat the gang or disobey other rules), and shorties (youngsters who staff drug-selling spots and execute drug deals).

Impact on Schools and Education

Where they have a substantial presence, youth gangs are linked with serious delinquency problems in elementary and secondary schools in the United States. This study of data gathered in the School Crime Supplement to the 1995 National Crime Victim Survey documented several examples. First, there is a strong correlation between gang presence in schools and both guns in schools and availability of drugs in school. Second, higher percentages of students report knowing a student who brought a gun to school when students report gang presence (25%) than when gangs were not present (8%).

In addition, gang presence at a student's school is related to seeing a student with a gun at school: 12% report having seen a student with a gun in school when gangs are present versus 3% when gangs are not present. Third, students who report that any drugs (marijuana, cocaine, crack, or uppers/downers) are readily available at school are much more likely to report gangs at their school (35%) than those who say that no drugs are available (14%). Fourth, the presence of gangs more than doubles the likelihood of violent victimization at school (nearly 8% vs. 3%).

The presence of street gangs at school also can be very disruptive to the school environment because they may not only create fear among students but also increase the level of violence in schools. Gang presence is also an important contributor to overall levels of student victimization at school.

In the School Crime Supplement to the 2003 National Crime Victimization Survey, students, ages 12–18, were asked if street gangs were present at their schools during the previous six months. In 2003, 21% of students reported that there were gangs at their schools. However, no difference was detected between 2001 and 2003 in percentages of students who reported the presence of street gangs, regardless of school location. Of all the students surveyed, students in urban schools were the most likely to report the presence of street gangs at their school (31%), followed by suburban students and rural students, who were the least likely to do so (18% and 12%, respectively).

Greater security measures have been taken by school administrations in response to the gang problem, but the effectiveness of them is subject to debate. [In a 2000 study of gangs and school violence, researcher D.E. Thompkins wrote,] "The presence of security officers, metal detectors, and security cameras may deter some students from committing acts of violence, but this presence also serves to heighten fear among students and teachers, while increasing the power of some gangs and the perceived need some students have for joining gangs". It is also important to be aware that school-related gang crime extends beyond the boundaries of school buildings to contexts in which youths congregate before and after school hours; in fact, gang crime begins to escalate very early on school days.

Impact of Gang Involvement

Most youths who join gangs have already been involved in delinquency and drug use. Once in the gang, they are quite likely to become more actively involved in delinquency, drug use, and violence—and they are more likely to be victimized themselves. Their problems do not end here. They are at greater risk of arrest, juvenile court referral, detention, confinement in a juvenile correctional facility, and, later, imprisonment.

Gang involvement dramatically alters youngsters' life chances—particularly if they remain active in the gang for several years. Over and above embedding its members in criminal activity, the gang acts as "a powerful social network" in constraining the behavior of members, limiting access to prosocial networks, and cutting individuals off from conventional pursuits. These effects of the gang tend to produce precocious, off-time, and unsuccessful transitions that bring disorder to the life course in a cascading series of difficulties, including school dropout, early pregnancy or early impregnation, teen motherhood, and unstable employment. . . .

The Scope of Gang Impact

Some youth gangs are not actively involved in criminal acts—particularly not violent crimes. However, as one moves from small towns and rural areas to large cities, and particularly to our nation's largest cities, far more gang crime is seen. The economic impact of gangs is also far greater in these areas, with a far greater deleterious impact on communities in cities of 100,000 or more population. The very largest cities—with populations of 250,000 and above—report on average more than 30 gangs, more gang members, and far more gang-related homicides than less-populated cities.

The disproportionate impact of gang members' criminal activity on our communities is evident in several ways. First, gang members account for more than their share of crimes. Second, youths commit more crimes during the period of active involvement in a gang than during periods before joining and after leaving a gang. Third, gang members commit more serious crimes than other groups. Fourth, the criminal involvement of youths who remain in a gang for more than a year is long-lasting.

Overall, the impact of youth gangs on communities is felt in many ways. Intimidation of other youths, adults, witnesses, and business owners is not uncommon. Once the enormous numbers of homicides in Chicago and Los Angeles are factored in, more than one-fourth of all the homicides across the country are considered gang-related. Gang immigration may be a factor of greater importance than gang migration, in terms of the impact of outsiders on local gangs. The MS-13 gang may be an example of this, although its numbers are likely exaggerated in the broadcast media. On the other hand, gangs in schools are likely underestimated.

In general, law enforcement agencies tend to underreport gang incidents, and their estimates of the number of gangs and gang members are likely to overlook substantial numbers of students. Last, gangs tend to propel youths into a life of crime, punctuated by arrests, convictions, and periods of incarceration. The costs to society are enormous. Each assault-related gunshot injury costs the public approximately $1 million. A single adolescent criminal career of about ten years can cost taxpayers between $1.7 and $2.3 million.

Regardless of population size, any community that senses that it is experiencing a youth gang problem needs to undertake a thorough, objective, and comprehensive assessment.

THREE

Gangs Create Community for Members

John Seita

> Young people need to feel accepted as part of a group, John Seita argues. Seita notes that social clubs, school affiliations, and sports teams can provide a sense of belonging for youths. When these programs do not exist, or are not open to all young people, some youths will join street gangs to find connection with peers, he contends. Communities must provide alternatives to gang membership for young people looking for a sense of belonging and purpose, Seita maintains.
>
> John Seita is a professor of social work at Michigan State University. He specializes in working with at-risk and behaviorally challenged youth and has written several books on youth development.

As someone knowledgeable in youth development, resilience and community mobilization, I am both disappointed and, sadly, somewhat bemused that we seemingly do not understand the nature of gang formation.

Before I comment further on my disappointment . . ., let me note the variety and prevalence of gangs in Battle Creek [Michigan]. . . . Two local gangs are called "MOB vs. CMB," which is shorthand for Money Over Bitches vs. Cash Money

John Seita, "Young People Need Sense of Belonging, Purpose," *Battle Creek Enquirer*, February 4, 2007. www.battlecreekenquirer.com. Reproduced by permission.

Bailers. Let's be quick to note that there are other gangs in Battle Creek as well . . . .

For example, youth gangs in the Battle Creek area include Michigan State University's Extension 4-H program, school-based academic honor societies, school-based chess clubs and sports programs with which youth participate. There are other "gangs" as well.

There are even some adult gangs in Battle Creek. The Battle Creek Rotary Club, the Battle Creek AMBUCS and the Battle Creek Optimists are all gangs of sorts, too. If I forgot your gang, please forgive me, there are too many gangs in Battle Creek to mention. Oh, I also joined a gang. I am on the governing board of Summit Pointe, so I guess that makes me a member of the Summit Pointe gang.

I compare the various local service organizations to the more traditionally feared youth gangs in order to identify their similarities and their differences. Let's start with the similarities.

Gangs Provide a Sense of Belonging

All group membership, no matter the label given, is motivated by the need to belong and to be connected to other humans. Our survival as a species from the beginning of time was dependent upon tribal membership and being part of a "gang."

Adults join gangs/service groups for affiliation and for belonging. Youth join street gangs for affiliation and for belonging. Adults join professional groups to network. Youth join street gangs for the same reason. Adults join professional groups for purpose, and youth join street gangs for the same reason. There are too many similar motivations between adult and youth group membership to note in a short opinion column, but each reader can identify other similarities as well.

Let me be quick to add that there are also differences in motivation between joining [a] professional service organization and youth gang membership. Service groups are formed to better the community, whereas street gangs don't have that kind of mission. Community service groups are typically peaceable, whereas gangs are sometimes violent. Service groups are typically help-ful, whereas street gangs are often harmful. Again, each reader can identify other differences between street gangs and service clubs.

Earlier I noted that I am disappointed and bemused about how we view gangs in Battle Creek. I am disappointed that as a community we fail to understand what decades of research has revealed about youth development: Young people join gangs when they feel that they are no longer welcome or successful in mainstream society.

Jailed twice since he dropped out of high school, Rico Simpson now wants to earn a GED and receive job training. Some argue that dropouts join gangs in search of belonging, pur-pose, and direction, which they haven't received from main-stream society.

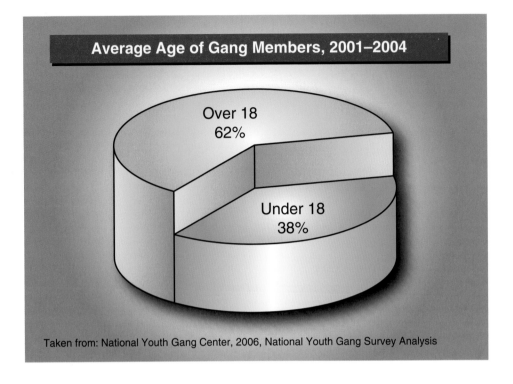

Average Age of Gang Members, 2001–2004

Over 18
62%

Under 18
38%

Taken from: National Youth Gang Center, 2006, National Youth Gang Survey Analysis

Gangs Provide a Substitute Family

Young people, who fail in school or are rejected by school peers or drop out of school, will reach beyond their families in search of substitute belongings with peers. Peer influence is often seen as negative because it is such a potent force in the lives of young persons, but peer bonding meets a powerful social need, and, generally, it is a positive process, even among delinquents. Youths weakly bonded to family and school are highly vulnerable to gang membership.

Even in prison, one keeps sanity by bonding to fellow inmates since the most powerful punishment is segregation. Just because a youth has questionable associates does not mean all values are anti-social. Studies show that most delinquent youth affirm positive values and would like to have positive friends. However, delinquent peer groups encourage delinquent values and high-risk behaviors as youths perform for their friends.

Youths compensate for problems elsewhere in their lives by joining with peers. If these friends are part of a delinquent or drug culture, the youth is propelled toward law-breaking behavior. The values of negative youth subcultures are often at odds with those of adults. Most delinquent young men lack positive male role models.

Community Alternatives Can Prevent Gangs

Therefore, rather than fear gangs, we ought to acknowledge that, as a community, gangs have outsmarted us. Gangs are providing what we, as a community, seem unable to provide for all of our young people: belonging, purpose, affiliation and acceptance. Until we work harder as a community to meet the basic developmental needs of all young people, fearsome youth gangs will meet those needs, and will only maintain and grow in our community. Don't be scared, be involved!

FOUR

Gangs Are
an Urban Problem

Howard N. Snyder and Melissa Sickmund

Gang activity in suburban and rural areas decreased between 1994 and 2004, but gangs in urban areas continued to present problems, argue Howard N. Snyder and Melissa Sickmund in the following viewpoint. While gang membership can be difficult to estimate and track over time, certain risk factors seem to determine the likelihood of a young person's gang involvement, the authors assert. Those who join gangs are more likely to commit serious crimes and become victims of violence themselves, and a large majority of cities continue to have problems with gangs and gang-related crime, the authors maintain.

Howard N. Snyder is the director of systems research at the National Center for Juvenile Justice. His research and analysis of juvenile crime, victimization, and corrections have appeared in numerous publications.

Melissa Sickmund is a senior research associate at the National Center for Juvenile Justice. Her work has focused on statistical information and the study of juvenile justice issues, particularly juveniles in the criminal court system.

Accurately estimating the scope of the youth gang problem is difficult in part because of the lack of consensus about what "counts"—what combination of size, stability, hierarchy, symbolic communication, and ongoing criminal activity distinguishes a true gang from a transitory collection of individuals, not to mention what level of involvement in and adherence to the gang distinguishes a real member from a hanger-on or "wannabe." In addition, the available sources of information on gangs are unreliable. Gangs are, after all, inherently secret groups. Outsiders are apt to miss or misinterpret signs of their presence. Insiders are liable to distort the signs.

Nevertheless, based on surveys of local authorities, it appears that the overall number of communities with active youth gangs grew sharply during the last few decades of the 20th century, peaked in the mid-1990s, and recently declined somewhat.

Gangs Are Less Persistent in Suburbs

A comparison of the number of localities reporting problems with youth gangs during the 1970s with the number reporting gang problems in the 1990s found a tenfold increase in gang jurisdictions—including more suburban, small-town, and rural jurisdictions with reported gang problems than ever before. On the basis of law enforcement agency responses to the 1996 National Youth Gang Survey, which gathered data on gangs from a representative sample of police and sheriff departments across the country, the nation's total youth gang membership was estimated at more than 846,000, with 31,000 gangs operating in 4,824 local jurisdictions.

Estimates based on subsequent surveys have steadily receded from those highs. Based on the 2004 survey, youth gang membership was estimated at 760,000 and total youth gangs at 24,000. Youth gangs were estimated to be active in more than 2,900 jurisdictions served by city (population of 2,500 or more) and county law enforcement agencies.

The drop between 1996 and 2004 in the number of localities reporting gang problems was almost entirely attributable to small cities and suburban and rural jurisdictions—where gang problems had tended to be relatively minor and less persistent. Nearly 8 in 10 cities with populations of 50,000 or more continued to report gang problems. Thus, most Americans still live in or near areas that have problems with youth gangs.

Gang Activity Is Related to Community Size

In a 1999–2000 survey of a nationally representative sample of public school principals, 18% reported "undesirable gang activities" in their schools—including 31% of the middle school and 37% of the secondary school principals. Apart from being more common in schools located in urban areas, in poor communities, and in communities with large minority populations, gang activity was strongly linked with school size: principals of schools with enrollments of 1,000 or more were about 4 times more likely to report gang activity than those with enrollments of less than 500.

In 2001 and again in 2003, as part of the School Crime Supplement to the National Crime Victimization Survey, students ages 12–18 were asked about the presence of gangs in their schools during the prior 6 months. In both years, about 1 in 5 reported that gangs were present. Among minority students, students in city schools, and those in upper grades, much higher proportions reported gang presence. For instance, in 2003, 42% of urban Hispanic students said they attended schools in which gangs were present.

Gang Membership Is Difficult to Measure

Law enforcement agencies responding to National Youth Gang Surveys over a number of years have reported demographic details regarding gang members in their jurisdictions, including age, gender, and racial and ethnic background. Although reported characteristics varied considerably by locality—with emergent gangs in less populous areas tending to have more white and more female members—overall, gang demographics have been fairly consistent from year to year.

On the basis of responses to the 2004 survey, gang membership was estimated to be 94% male. Youth gang membership was estimated to consist of 41% juveniles and 59% young adults (18 or older).

Gang demographic profiles based on law enforcement estimates differ from profiles emerging from youth surveys. Self-reported gang members tend to include many more females and nonminority males. For example, in one large-scale 1995 survey of public school 8th graders, 25% of self-reported gang members were white and 38% were female. Even when more restrictive criteria for gang membership were applied to these self-report results—in an effort to filter out fringe or inactive members and isolate only the most active core gang members—significant demographic differences from law enforcement estimates persisted.

Law enforcement estimates of nationwide juvenile gang membership suggest that no more than about 1% of all youth ages 10–17 are gang members. Self-reports, such as the 1997 National Longitudinal Survey of Youth (NLSY97), find that 2% of youth ages 12–17 (3% of males and 1% of females) say they were in a gang in the past year. NLSY97 also found that 8% of 17-year-olds (11% of males and 6% of females) said they had ever belonged to a gang. These proportions obviously vary considerably from place to place. For example, researchers tracking a sample of high-risk youth in Rochester, NY, reported that 30% joined gangs between the ages of 14 and 18.

Gang membership tends to be short-lived, even among high-risk youth. Among the Rochester gang members, half of the males and two-thirds of the females stayed in gangs for a year or less, with very few youth remaining gang members throughout their adolescent years.

Who Is Likely to Join a Gang?

When asked directly, what led them to join gangs, 54% of Rochester gang members said they had followed the lead of friends or family members who preceded them, 19% said they did it for protection, and 15% said it was for fun or excitement. Younger gang members were somewhat more likely to cite protection as the primary motivation.

However they may characterize their own motivations, gang members' backgrounds commonly include certain features that may make them more inclined to join gangs. The following risk factors have been found to predict gang membership:

- Individual factors: early delinquency (especially violence and drug use) and early dating and precocious sexual activity.
- Family factors: non-two-parent structure, poverty, and other gang-involved members.
- School factors: low achievement, commitment, and aspirations; truancy; negative labeling by teachers; and lack of a sense of safety in school.
- Peer factors: associations with delinquent or aggressive peers.
- Community factors: poverty, drug availability, gang presence, lack of a sense of safety and attachment.

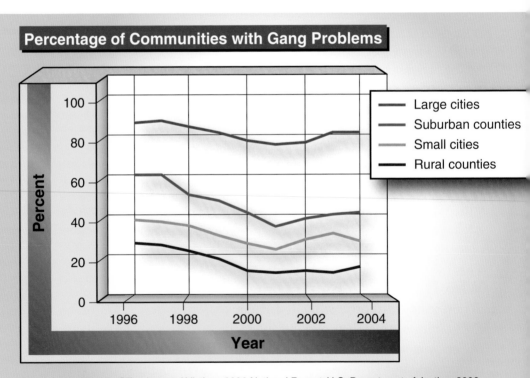

Percentage of Communities with Gang Problems

Taken from: *Juvenile Offenders and Victims: 2006 National Report*, U.S. Department of Justice, 2006

Some risk factors are more predictive than others. In a longitudinal study of youth living in high-crime neighborhoods in Seattle, for example, pre-adolescents (ages 10–12) who later joined gangs were distinguished most markedly by very early marijuana use, neighborhood conditions making marijuana readily available, and learning disabilities. The presence of any of these factors in a juvenile's background more than tripled the odds of his or her later becoming a gang member. Childhood risk factors that were predictive of later sustained (as opposed to transient) gang membership included early violence, acting out, and association with antisocial peers.

The more risk factors present in a youth's background, the more likely that youth is to join a gang. In Seattle, for example, those with two or three identified risk factors at ages 10–12 were 3 times more likely to go on to join a gang than those with none or one, those with four to six risk factors were 5 times more likely, and those with seven or more were 13 times more likely. Having background risk factors in more than one area of life—that is, individual, family, community, etc.—increases the likelihood of gang involvement even more man a general accumulation of factors. The Rochester study, which divided risk factors into seven general domains, found that 61% of the boys and 40% of the girls with problems in all seven areas were gang members.

Gang Members Commit More Crimes than Other Youths

By their own account, gang members are more likely to engage in criminal activity than their peers. In response to interview questions regarding their activities in the prior month, Seattle gang members were 3 times more likely than nongang members to report committing break-ins and assaults, 4 times more likely to report committing felony thefts, and 8 times more likely to report committing robberies. When asked about their activities during the prior year, gang members were 3 times more likely to say they had been arrested, and 5 times more likely to say they had sold drugs.

A bloodstain marks the sidewalk in Houston's Ervan Chew Park, the result of a brutal gang beating and stabbing that left a fourteen-year-old dead.

In surveys of high-risk youth, gang members represent a minority of these youth but account for most of the reported crime. In the Rochester study, gang members made up 30% of the sample but accounted for 54% of the arrests, 68% of the property crimes, 69% of the violent offenses, 70% of the drug sales, and 82% of the serious delinquencies. A similar study of high-risk Denver youth found that gang members constituted just 14% of the sample but committed 80% of the serious and violent crimes. . . .

Gang members have been found to be more criminally active and violent than delinquents who are not gang affiliated, even those who associate to the same extent with other delinquents. Furthermore, this heightened criminality and violence occur only during periods of gang membership—not before or after. Rochester juveniles who were gang members during only 1 year between ages 14 and 18 committed more offenses during that 1 gang year than they did in any of the remaining 3 years, Denver youth involved in gangs over some part of a 5-year period committed 85% of their serious violent offenses, 86% of their serious property offenses, and 80% of their drug sales while gang-involved. All of these findings strongly suggest that the gang structure itself tends to facilitate or even demand increased involvement in delinquency.

Gangs and Guns

A significant factor may be the strong association between gang membership and gun possession. Gang members are far more likely than nonmembers to own or have access to guns, to carry them on the street, and to use them to commit crimes. Gang membership both facilitates juveniles' access to guns—through illegal markets and through borrowing—and provides strong and constant incentives for being armed in public. Rochester gang members' rates of gun-carrying were 10 times higher than those of nonmembers. For these youth, gun-carrying not only multiplies opportunities to commit violent crimes and raises the risk that ordinary disputes will escalate into violence—it may increase a youth's crime-readiness by supplying an all-purpose, aggressive confidence that unarmed youth do not have.

Being a member of a gang sharply raises a young person's risk of being a victim of violence, not just a perpetrator. Gangs may harm members in subtle as well as obvious ways, cutting them off from people and opportunities that could help them with the transition to adulthood and disrupting their lives even after they have moved beyond the gang.

Researchers tracking the lives of Rochester gang members to age 22 found evidence of serious adult dysfunction that could not be explained by other factors. Young adults who had been in gangs were more likely to have ended their education prematurely, become pregnant or had children early, and failed to establish stable work lives—all of which were associated with an increased likelihood of being arrested as adults. The differences were more notable among those who had been in gangs for a long time and persisted even when gang members were compared with non-members who had histories of delinquency and association with delinquent peers.

FIVE

Gangs Are a Suburban and Rural Problem

Mark Sappenfield

Normally, when people think of gangs, they think of big cities, states Mark Sappenfield in the following selection. But gangs are moving into rural America. All over the country, what used to be quiet, safe, rural, and suburban towns are now being faced with increased crime and fear, asserts Sappenfield. Recognition of increased gang activity in nonurban areas is needed, along with increased public awareness and effective policing strategies, the author maintains.

Mark Sappenfield is a staff writer for the *Christian Science Monitor*, a national daily newspaper.

Glenn County is hardly a place that conjures up images of gang violence. This is a land scratched from the tender Sacramento Valley earth in endless rows of almond trees, nodding fields of wheat, and plains as flat and hot as a baking sheet.

Along Interstate 5 North, it is a rest stop on the way to no place in particular. In an area larger than Rhode Island, there are seven stoplights.

Yet it is here, in this isolated agricultural cradle, that someone stopping for gas was chased and stabbed for wearing rival gang colors. It is here that a teen was killed in a shooting at the local cinema.

The stories are the same across the iron belt of upper Minnesota, the cornfields of Illinois, and the alpine valleys of Utah. Rural America has a gang problem.

What began a decade ago with the widening of the drug trade and the migration of many gang members has now taken root in

Orena Hernandez has just learned that her boyfriend was killed in a drive-by shooting. Gang violence, once associated with inner cities, has spread throughout the United States.

the heartland. Searching for a sense of belonging and the trappings of a seemingly more exciting urban life, farm workers' sons and high-school dropouts have swelled the ranks of rural gangs, bringing street fights and shootings to areas that had only seen such things on "NYPD Blue."

Raising Awareness

While gangs remain a more pressing problem in cities, their spread into even the most remote niches of America has upended the small-town idyll of communities nationwide. As a result, these towns are transforming their law-enforcement efforts, seeing gangs as a primary public-safety concern.

"There has been much more activity in rural areas . . . in the past 10 years," says Walter Miller, a consultant to the US Department of Justice in Cambridge, Mass.

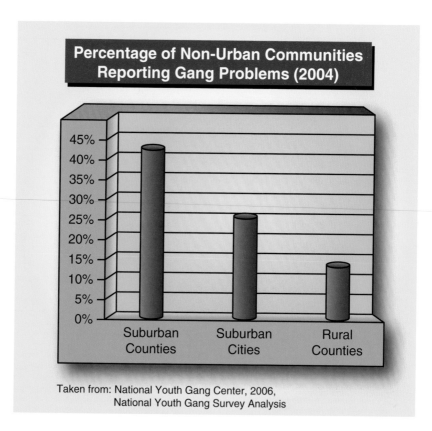

Percentage of Non-Urban Communities Reporting Gang Problems (2004)

Taken from: National Youth Gang Center, 2006,
National Youth Gang Survey Analysis

He himself documented the trend in one study for the Justice Department that traced youth gangs from 1970 to 1998. Most notably, 41 percent more cities with populations between 1,000 to 2,500 people saw gangs arrive by 1998.

The reasons for the jump vary from region to region. In Midwestern towns, law-enforcement officials say gangs in Chicago and Minneapolis have spread their crack-cocaine trade farther beyond beltways. "It's all price driven," says Jim Wright of the Minnesota Gang Strike Force in Duluth. "If you can drive five or six hours and make five times more money, you're going to do it."

The last two murders there have been gang-related, and when a gang member went on trial across the border in Wisconsin, the prosecutor's house was firebombed. In Mount Vernon, Ill., at the height of its gang problem in 1994, the community of 17,000 had six homicides.

Rural Gangs Flourish

Yet in many parts of the West, gangs seem to have flourished for a different reason: boredom. Here in Glenn County, where a trip to the big city means driving to Chico, gangs offer something to do—an escape from the agricultural depression that grips the county.

Authorities first started seeing gang graffiti in the early 1990s. Since then, a dozen gangs have sprouted among the 27,000 residents. Most are overwhelmingly Hispanic, and for these youths, the county is divided as clearly as Belfast [Northern Ireland is between Catholics and Protestants]. Orland and Hamilton City are split between the Surenos and the Nortenos—two Mexican gangs born in San Quentin prison in 1968. According to legend, a member of the Surenos moved to Orland, and a Hamilton City resident returned from prison as a Norteno, beginning the rivalry.

It's a typical pattern, says Joan Liquin of the Logan-Cache County Gang Project in Utah. Migration of gang members—either voluntarily or through juvenile-relocation programs—has spurred the growth of gangs in her area. In four years, the number of gang members there has risen from 45 to 330. As in Glenn County, most gang-related crimes have been minor: Thefts, vandalism, and fistfights top the list.

Helping At-Risk Teens

These are charges that Francisco knows well. But the teen hardly seems like a gang-banger. For one, he smiles too much. In fact, he's good-natured and laughing, even when talking about run-ins with the police as a member of the Surenos.

He talks in past tense, though, because—with the help of Glenn County's Project Exito—he has dropped out.

"I just got tired of always getting in trouble," says Francisco (not his real name). "Half the guys I used to hang out with don't like me anymore. . . . But last time I got out of juvenile hall, I got tired of being there."

Standing nearby, Sal Hernandez and Ulises Tellechea long to hear these words more often. While the federally funded program brings together all sorts of people—from teachers to probation officers—to help at-risk teens, Messrs. Hernandez and Tellechea have the task of befriending as many gang members as possible.

In essence, their job is to hang out. On this day, they drive through Orland on the way to shoot hoops with some students in Hamilton City. At every stop, they talk to as many kids as they can. They plan activities for anyone who wants to come along—with the knowledge that gang ties are left behind.

They've taken one group to a Latino youth leadership conference and another to San Francisco to see Alcatraz and a baseball game. One weekend, they went camping in the foothills of the Sierra Nevada. The goal is to create mutual trust, and show kids a life beyond gangs.

There are setbacks, Tellechea says, like when a teen he's working with ends up back in juvenile hall—not to mention the fact that Orland and Hamilton City kids still won't do anything together. But many signs are positive, both here and nationwide.

National statistics suggest that rural gang activity peaked in the mid-1990s and is gradually declining. In Glenn County, law-enforcement officials see less graffiti and violence. . . .

And Tellechea is also seeing a difference. "One of the kids asked me to go shopping because he didn't want to wear his gang clothes anymore," he says. "He said, 'I want to dress like you.'"

SIX

Hip-Hop Culture Promotes Gangs

Chip Johnson

Chip Johnson is a columnist for the *San Francisco Chronicle* newspaper.

Hip-hop music often depicts a dangerous, violent gang-ster lifestyle that is emulated by young people across the United States, argues Chip Johnson in the following viewpoint. Music videos, rap lyrics, clothing, jewelry, and other merchandise support hip-hop culture and sometimes become gang symbols, he states. Johnson contends that young people adopt hip-hop style because it is fashionable and trendy, but some young people also copy the gangster behavior shown in many hip-hop music videos. Music and clothing companies who promote gangster style and behavior are making the nation's gang problems worse, Johnson maintains.

The carnage on the streets of Oakland [California] these days just doesn't make any sense as the body count of youths—particularly black teenagers—mounts.

[In August 2006], controversial civil rights activist the Rev. Al Sharpton, in a keynote address at the annual National Association of Black Journalists conference in Indianapolis, warned of the dangers of doing nothing about the glorification of the gangster lifestyle.

"We have got to get out of this gangster mentality, acting as if gangsterism and blackness are synonymous," Sharpton said.

"I think we have allowed a whole generation of young people to feel that if they're focused, they're not black enough. If they speak well and act well, they're acting white, and there's nothing more racist than that."

A member of the Grape Street Crips gang displays a tattoo on his back that reads "Tha Good Die Young."

I'm not a big Sharpton supporter, given some of his more extreme viewpoints, but I agree with him on this one. Heck, 10 years ago, the Rev. Calvin Butts of the Abyssinian Baptist Church in Harlem said the same thing about the alarming trends in violent gangster rap music, but he was dismissed as a religious conservative.

Gangster Musicians Promote Violence

There isn't a city in the continental United States where teenagers have embraced the message of the gangster musician with more zeal than in Oakland, which has produced some of the most notable artists who make up the genre today.

Unfortunately, the lifestyle glorified in the music videos is a dicey proposition in urban America, because some of our young people aren't just playing it—they're living it.

Consider [one] Oakland . . . homicide, its 89th of [2006]: the drive-by shooting death of Andrew Porter, a 16-year-old junior at Oakland High School. He was killed in a hail of bullets late [one] Saturday night while walking with a large group of people to a party on 81st Avenue.

While Andrew's mother said her son, a starter on his high school football team, was a good kid who was not involved in crime, a different—and threatening—picture of his purported circle of friends emerged on a Web site.

The posting on myspace.com honors his death—and vows revenge.

The site, which appears to be devoted to an Oakland street gang, includes this: "RIP Andrew—Mob Squad—We go get who did it bra." The site includes links to chat rooms, message boards and other Internet locations.

Andrew Porter is the 27th of Oakland's 89 homicide victims [in 2006] who have died short of their 20th birthday. That's nearly 1 out of 3.

Some of the photographs on the Web site show teens throwing up a three-finger gang sign, while others brandish handguns. One rolling image, headlined "Foothill Fruitville," shows a man holding two automatic pistols, one in each hand.

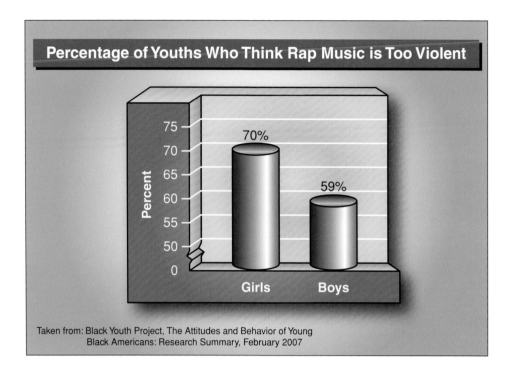

Percentage of Youths Who Think Rap Music is Too Violent

70%

59%

Percent

Girls   Boys

Taken from: Black Youth Project, The Attitudes and Behavior of Young
Black Americans: Research Summary, February 2007

Another part of the site is set aside for slain members of the group, and includes the faces and names of at least two other African American teens from Oakland who have been gunned down [from 2004 to 2006].

Davelle Tatum was just 16 when gunmen—waiting for him to arrive home—opened fire in June 2005, killing him. A separate memorial was posted to note the death of Willie Clay, 19, who died when someone fired on a group of people near the corner of 22nd Avenue and East 28th Street, for years a known drug hotspot.

Three days after Clay's death, Purnell Brewer, a well-known and feared street drug dealer, was gunned down on 26th Street nearby.

The MySpace site is ostensibly dedicated to the members of a gang whose turf . . . is known to authorities as the area around 22nd Avenue between East 21st and 29th streets where nearly a dozen people have been killed so far [in 2006].

Hip-Hop Merchandise Encourages Violence

What's particularly troubling, beyond the remarkably short lives of these young men, is that these teenagers and young adults operate the site so publicly, and have posted links to advertisements selling "Bling-bling" hip-hop jewelry and clothing—all the accoutrements that a budding young street thug will need.

Young black men, many of them without guidance or role models in their lives, are slipping from society's grasp faster than we can catch them. But it's particularly galling to see corporate America cashing in on the carnage.

I mean the record and fashion industries, and all the other companies promoting gangster-like behavior through the distribution of their products. It only makes matters worse.

The kids on the streets of Oakland and other cities are just going along with what's hip and cool, which is the exact same thing my generation did 30 years ago, whether it was smoking pot, sporting a freakin' fro or hanging with the bad dudes.

And just like us, many of the kids who find themselves caught up in a real-life gangster drama may have just been playing at first.

But for anybody who's had their head in the sand, playing street thug in the nation's toughest inner cities, including Oakland, ain't no game, man.

SEVEN

Hip-Hop Music Can Discourage Gang Activity

Sara Libby

> Hip-hop music does much more than just promote violence, sexism, and gang activity; its messages can inspire people to better themselves and the world around them, argues Sara Libby in the following viewpoint. Critics have narrowed their views of rap music to the inappropriate and violent songs while ignoring the fact that young people are being empowered by the love and respect often promoted in rap lyrics, Libby maintains. Hip-hop has the ability to bring communities together, promoting culture and arts, she concludes.
>
> Sara Libby is an editor for Creators Syndicate, an agency for writers and artists.

In the aftermath of the Don Imus debacle [in his April 4, 2007, radio show, Imus referred to players of the Rutgers University women's basketball team as "nappy-headed hos."], everyone from conservative pundits to rap mogul Russell Simmons has pointed a finger at hip-hop, arguing that while Mr. Imus's rant was inappropriate, rap stars get away with such sexist and racially charged language on a daily basis. And sure, there are plenty of rap songs that celebrate homophobia, intolerance, and women-bashing. But

Sara Libby, "Hip-Hop's Bad Rap," *Christian Science Monitor*, May 3, 2007. Reproduced by permission of the author.

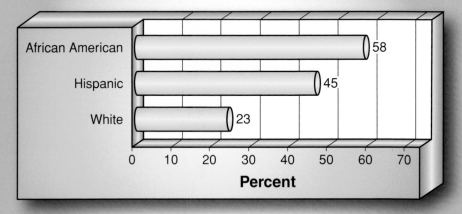

Percentage of Youths Who Listen to Rap Music Every Day

African American — 58
Hispanic — 45
White — 23

Percent

Taken from: Black Youth Project, The Attitudes and Behavior of Young
Black Americans: Research Summary, February 2007

to say that hip-hop comprises only those qualities is like saying that country artists croon solely about pickup trucks.

I grew up in virtually all-white McMinnville, Ore., and, save for the occasional minority scholarship I didn't qualify for, have never been discriminated against. Yet, thanks to the magic of MTV, I became transfixed by hip-hop at an early age—begging my mom for rides to the local record store to pick up releases by LL Cool J, Dr. Dre, and the Beastie Boys. In each album, I found something familiar and relatable. In the gangstas trying to escape the violence of Compton, Calif., I saw myself wanting out of a small, stifling farm town; their rants against the police reminded me of teachers and others who never took the time to understand my perspective.

The fact that I—a petite, well-educated blond woman—am rushing to defend rap music should at least make you think twice before condemning hip-hop as a genre that celebrates violence and sexism.

Rapper Ludacris (right) talks with singers Lyfe Jennings and Shareefa at an event to teach high-school students about music industry jobs, just one example of how hip-hop artists make positive contributions to society.

Rap Music Inspires

Never once did listening to rap make me run out and buy a gun or sleep around. Rather, I was empowered by Salt-N-Pepa telling me "fight for your rights, stand up and be heard/ you're just as good as any man, believe that, word" and impressed by Tupac Shakur's willingness to rap unabashedly about his love for his mama.

When I moved to Los Angeles for college, I joined other young intellectuals in classes on black pop culture and black literature, where I was often the only white student. I was inspired to study the lynching of Emmett Till after hearing him mentioned not by Bob Dylan, but in a song by rapper Kanye West.

Opponents of Rap

Which is why I've been dumbfounded by critics who have recently characterized rap as strictly the domain of materialists and misogynists. Honestly, has [conservative news commentator]

Bill O'Reilly ever actually sat down and listened to a single rap song in its entirety? (Disclosure: I work for the company that syndicates his column.) The pundit's favorite whipping boy has been the rapper Ludacris, whom he lambastes for using profanity and referencing violence. But the last time I checked, Ludacris's recent hit was "Runaway Love," in which he spotlights domestic violence against women with concern and care.

When I go on my daily afternoon run, the first song on my workout mix is "I Can" by Nas, in which he addresses young blacks, telling them: "Nobody says you have to be gangstas, hos/ read more, learn more, change the globe." And just this morning, I heard a radio commercial by rapper Nick Cannon, who also hosts a hip-hop-themed show on MTV, imploring young people to check out community college as a way to better themselves.

Rap's Underlying Message

Another one of [2006–2007]'s best-selling rap artists, T.I., seduces a woman on the song "Why You Wanna" not by saying he wants to slap her behind, but by offering to "compliment you on your intellect and treat you wit respect." Yes, the lyrics are punctuated by R-rated language and imagery, but there's a critical difference between a song's profanity and its underlying message.

Some would argue—perhaps rightly so—that using terms such as "ho" and the "N" word is never OK, no matter what the context. But rap, like all music, is simply a reflection of the society that gave rise to it—and America's in particular is one with a centuries-old history of relegating blacks and women to the bottom of the barrel, something white men were practicing long before the Sugar Hill Gang and other early rap groups came along.

If hip-hop detractors really cared about the generation they insist is being corrupted, they should also acknowledge the surprising amount of good that hip-hop does as a vehicle that opens young people's eyes to poetry and dance. It's a medium that pleads for its audience to take part in their communities—and one that increasingly affirms women as teachers and role models.

EIGHT

The Number of Girls in Gangs Is Increasing

Mars Eghigian and Katherine Kirby

> Girls join gangs for many of the same reasons that boys
> do, and the number of girls in gangs is growing, assert the
> authors of the following viewpoint. Some girls begin par-
> ticipating in gang activity as early as age eight, the authors
> point out. Girls are most often auxiliary members of male
> gangs, but coed and female gangs are becoming more com-
> mon, the authors contend. Most female gang members do
> not participate in violent crimes, the authors argue, but
> rather provide support services such as transporting, pur-
> chasing, or selling drugs and guns or conveying messages
> to gang members in prison. Gang intervention programs
> should focus on girls who are at risk of gang involvement,
> because it is critical that the growing participation of girls
> in gangs be addressed, the authors maintain.
>
> Mars Eghigian is an independent researcher and author
> who has published articles in numerous journals and maga-
> zines. Katherine Kirby is the executive vice president of
> the Chicago Crime Commission, a not-for-profit organiza-
> tion dedicated to improving public safety in that city.

Biases, misconceptions and a general lack of awareness in the
past have led . . . a vast misreporting and underreporting of
female crime connected to street gangs. In 1999, Chicago Crime

Mars Eghigian and Katherine Kirby, "Girls in Gangs: On the Rise in America," *Corrections Today*, v. 68,
April 2006. Copyright © 2006 American Correctional Association, Inc. Reproduced by permission.

Commission researchers put the estimated number of female gang members in the Chicago area at 16,000 to 20,000. Mostly associates in the established male street gang, girls range from hardcore members to "groupies" looking for a good time and someplace to hang out.

Unfortunately, their numbers appear to be growing. Law enforcement has documented their participation in all forms of violence, and today they are appearing in "girls only" gangs. These gangs form from direct recruits or from the ranks of dissatisfied former members of male gangs looking for more opportunity.

Why Girls Join Gangs

Girls join gangs for the same reason most boys do—multiple factors and circumstances that have existed throughout their lives: financial opportunity, identity and status, peer pressure, family dysfunction and protection. However, some girls readily admit that they join because they are bored and look to gangs for a social life; they are looking for fun and excitement and a means to find parties and meet boys. Regrettably for those who naively join expecting harmless social rewards, they may find out too late about the actual violent nature of street gang existence. Still, others join simply because gangs are there in the neighborhood and are viewed as an everyday way of life. And perhaps the most disturbing impact of female association with street gang members is that eventually the relationship results in the birth of children—children who then grow up indoctrinated into the gang way of life.

What Girls Do in Gangs

It is not unheard of for girls to slide into gang involvement as early as age 8. Those who enter at this age and up to 10 years of age often have relatives who are gang members or have experienced a strong gang presence in their neighborhoods. At this age, the girl may begin to hang around the gang, learn gang culture, experiment with drugs and engage in low-level criminal activity.

Ages 11 and 12 represent the more likely age at which a girl may enter a gang, usually to gain recognition from older females. By then, they will begin skipping school, drinking, experimenting with drugs, performing low-level crimes and engaging in sexual activity.

The prime age at which females undergo their gang initiation appears to be around the ages of 13 and 14. Statistics show they are quite active in property crime such as larceny/theft, motor vehicle theft and burglary, as well as weapons offenses and violent assaults. They also are very likely engaging in sexual activity, and some are getting pregnant.

Ages 15 through 18 represent the hardcore years of female gang activity. Crimes committed such as robbery and aggravated assault peak at age 15 and remain consistently high through this age period. Murders peak at age 18.

Maria Ball (left) is one of the few female members in Yakima, Washington's Chicanos Por Vida gang. Her short haircut, tattoos, and piercings help prove her toughness to fellow gang members.

From age 19 and up, the female gang member faces several options. If she has children, she may assume responsibility for paying bills and caring for them. In order to do so, she may continue to sell drugs, go into prostitution or further participate in criminal activity. Indeed, statistics show that at this time female criminal activities peak in the form of white-collar crimes such as fraud, forgery and counterfeiting, and drug violations.

Another path may lead her to become a gang leader or adviser to young gang members. Younger girls will consider her to be an "OG" or "old gangster." She may be married to an active gang member and still socialize with and perform criminal acts for the gang. However, as she gets older, that activity will often dissipate. Quite possibly, an older female gang member will find legitimate employment and advance her education. Those who do usually develop different interests and friends, and as a result, they tend to drift away from their old gang and eventually leave it altogether.

Gang Initiation for Girls

Initiation requirements of a "wannabe" or outsider into the gang, marking full-fledged membership, may take several forms, depending on the particular gang. In some cases, the initiate may select the method; in others, it will be dictated to her. They can generally be classified into four types:

- "Violated" or "jumped in" refers to a physical beating the candidate must absorb to prove her toughness, loyalty and commitment to the gang;
- The mission method simply requires the girl to commit a criminal act, perhaps ride along on a drive-by shooting or even be dropped off deep in enemy territory and forced to get out alive;
- "Sexed in" is not the most common, but certainly the least respected initiation, in which a female may elect to participate in sex with a gang member. However, both girls and boys alike look down on this initiation, and those who elect this course are usually typecast and have extremely low status; and

- "Walked in" or "blessed in" is reserved only for those girls who have had generations of family as gang members, who have a family member in good gang standing, or who have grown up in the neighborhood, are well known, respected and have proved their loyalty beyond question.

Types of Gang Membership

Functions of women in gangs vary depending on the individual's personality and the dynamics of the gang she joins. Typically, she will fall into one of four membership categories:

- Auxiliary members of male gangs;
- A female member of a coed gang;
- Members of autonomous all-female gangs; or
- A female leader in a coed gang.

In Chicago, the vast majority of female gang members may be categorized as being auxiliary members of male gangs. Although a few may rise to be marginally independent of some male authority and set rules for other girls in the gang, they are usually of lower status, subservient to male gang objectives and, depending on the gang culture, are usually treated with little respect by their male peers, who in some gangs view them as weak. Nonetheless, they perform integral gang duties such as serving as lookouts and drug and weapons couriers, luring rivals for ambushes and providing alibis.

As members of a coed gang, the females may achieve much higher status because the males will entrust in them sensitive matters such as stashing drugs, weapons and money. In the latter, they may launder large amounts of cash for the gang. The females may also act as liaisons between the gang members on the streets and those in prison. Some authorities believe that they may be the primary players in bringing drugs into correctional facilities.

Female leaders within coed gangs usually retain authority over the female portion of the gang and seldom rise to equal their male counterparts when it comes to making decisions. A female leader usually has a bond with a high-ranking male or may be a family member or perhaps a long-time gang member who grew up in the neighborhood and who has proved her ability and loyalty beyond question. In some cases, she may actually run the business of a male counterpart if the latter is incarcerated.

Authorities believe that autonomous all-female gangs, while more common in Los Angeles, will be the next threat to Chicago youths. Auxiliary members of male gangs may tire of subordination and strike out on their own, assuming more authoritative roles. All-female groups do exist; however, they are not yet classified as true street gangs but are headed in that direction.

Party Crews and Wannabes

The most common group of women—party crews—comprises females who socialize and party together. They are not loyal to any

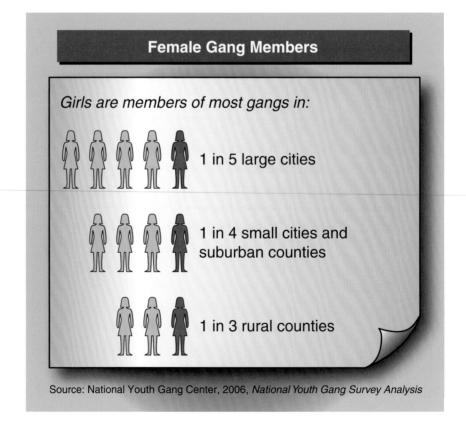

Female Gang Members

Girls are members of most gangs in:

1 in 5 large cities

1 in 4 small cities and suburban counties

1 in 3 rural counties

Source: National Youth Gang Center, 2006, *National Youth Gang Survey Analysis*

one gang but will go to whichever group is throwing the best parties or whomever they are most attracted to at any given moment. There are no rules, allegiances, rituals or hierarchy within the party crews. Benign as they might seem, regrettably, they put themselves in positions that may eventually provide the cohesion and tendencies common to street gangs.

For example, when a party crew infringes on the territory claimed by female auxiliary members of another gang, the party crew is forced to defend itself. Retaliations ensue, thus beginning the cycle of violence. In some cases, party crews have branched out into the sale of certain drugs. Unfortunately, the trade exposes them to extreme danger with established street gangs who have long organized and tightly controlled the trade. The party crews may then be forced to commit [an act of] loyalty to a gang, pay a street tax (to the gang for permission to sell drugs in its territory) or risk being killed.

Some girls appear to be gang members but are wannabes. More commonly referred to as groupies, they tag along with gang members, wear gang colors and sometimes engage in criminal activities but retain their independence and have not yet been through any formal initiation. This is usually the younger girls.

The Role of Girls in Gangs

The roles that girls in gangs may play are extensive and may include:

- Holding and transporting drugs and guns, as law enforcement are less likely to search women;
- Acting as information and contraband couriers to and from prisons;
- Finding strategic employment—infiltrating law enforcement or county clerk's offices to secure intelligence on gang member targets or witnesses acting against their own members, working for law firms in order to facilitate communications with members who are incarcerated, working for temp services and a host of other companies in order to get personal

information from the general public (e.g., credit card numbers) for white-collar fraud schemes, or working in bookstores in order to hide contraband (e.g., drugs) mailed to prison inmates;

- Acting as lures with rival gang members to secure information or set them up for a murder or a violent hit;
- Gangbanging and supporting criminal acts, including selling drugs, robbery, burglary, carjacking, car theft and drive-by shootings;
- Purchasing weapons;
- Hiding money; and/or
- Providing behind-the-scenes domestic support.

Leaving the Gang

All sectors of society must act now to keep female gangs from following in the footsteps of the powerful male gangs. It is unacceptable to wait until there is a devastating increase in the death, injury and imprisonment of the nation's young female populations. However, it is important to note that for those seeking to sever gang ties or those helping someone to sever ties, there are several considerations to take into account:

- Anyone seeking to leave must sincerely want to leave—no one can force her to quit;
- Girls should seek help from a trusted adult or network of trusted adults such as social workers, school officials, law enforcement officers, religious leaders and nongang-affiliated family members, etc.
- No gang is an individual and, as an organization, they have their own rules of conduct—one must clearly understand these rules when developing a strategy for a girl to exit the gang life or her life or well-being could be seriously jeopardized;
- A girl leaving must understand that her former enemies will still be enemies and that she will no longer have the protection of the gang;

- As the gang may be concerned about the girl's ability to share gang intelligence, careful planning must take place so that the gang is not able to permanently "silence" her;
- The entire family of a female gang member must be committed to the exit strategy or they also may be in extreme danger when left behind;
- Once the decision is made to exit the gang, the former gang member cannot return to the gang neighborhood; and
- If a former gang member does not move far away, there is always a chance she may run into gang members who will recognize her.

Although it may appear to a girl gang member that the gang provides her with protection, the reality is that when the exit is handled well, it is always safer to be out of a gang. Researchers, law enforcement agencies, health facilities and others must take steps to improve the tracking and data collection on female gang members, it is important that social service agencies, the faith community, parents and family, and others intervene early with troubled girls to provide them with positive opportunities and fill their basic life needs before they turn to gangs for support. Social service systems and others must increase and enhance programming for girls, and education systems need to implement effective school strategies such as dress codes. With adults and youths alike working in concert, the problem of girls in gangs can be reduced or even halted.

NINE

The Number of Immigrants in Gangs Is Increasing

Shelly Feuer Domash

One of the most serious gang problems in the United States today, argues Shelly Feuer Domash in the following viewpoint, is the growth of Mara Salvatrucha, better known as MS-13. This extremely violent gang first began in El Salvador and spread throughout Latin America and the United States. MS-13 members are primarily Hispanic immigrants, and their gang activity was previously limited to immigrant communities, Domash points out. But the gang has now become a serious threat in many parts of the country, she contends. Stronger antigang laws are needed in the United States as well as internationally in order to prevent future MS-13 violence, Domash maintains.

Shelly Feuer Domash is an independent journalist and writer. She has contributed articles to *Police* magazine, *Newsday*, the *New York Times*, and many other national publications. She has also coauthored a book, *Crime and the Media: Headlines vs. Reality*, and produced numerous documentaries on topics including gangs and drugs.

Within one hour, two people were found murdered miles apart in suburban Nassau County, N.Y. After an intensive investigation, police officials learned the murders were the work of the violent street gang Mara Salvatrucha 13. It also soon

Shelly Feuer Domash, "America's Most Dangerous Gang," *Police: The Law Enforcement Magazine*, February 2005. www.policemag.com. Reproduced by permission.

became apparent the gang was sending a bold message to its members and associates. That message: "If you are not loyal, you are dead."

But there was another message in the brutal slayings for the people of Long Island. And that message was that gang violence had moved into the upper middle class enclaves of the Island, into the kinds of communities where the locals assume that crime is somebody else's problem.

Mara Salvatrucha 13 (MS-13) is unfortunately becoming everybody's problem. This plague that came to Long Island from El Salvador by way of the streets of Los Angeles follows the same migratory patterns as the Salvadoran immigrant community that it preys upon, fanning out across the United States from ethnic enclaves in California.

Organized Crime

Until recently, MS-13 wasn't that big a player in East Coast gang culture. The reason for its weak position in the East Coast crime world was obvious: It wasn't very well organized. MS-13 was comprised of a group of cliques that operated independently of each other.

No more. Law enforcement officials now report that gang members from across the country have come together to unite affiliated groups up and down the East Coast. The leadership for these cliques is now coming from as far away as California and even from El Salvador.

Robert Hart, senior agent in charge with the FBI, says that when individual groups of MS-13 unite, the results can be devastating. "The cliques, instead of operating independently of each other, are beginning to come together," Hart explains. "The difference is by doing that, obviously you have a much tighter organization, much stronger structures and, instead of having various cliques doing whatever they want, wherever they want, there is one individual who is the leader and is able to control the payment of dues and the criminal acts they engage in. The result is very, very similar to what you would see in what we refer to as traditional organized criminal families."

Gang Migration

Los Angeles and New York law enforcement and even politicians are aware of the impact of MS-13 on their streets and on their crime statistics. So they've taken action. The results are usually not stellar, but at least these cities have recognized that MS-13 is a problem. Unfortunately, the leadership of MS-13 is not stupid. Once the heat comes down hard in L.A. and New York, they head for new turf, choosing Midwestern and Southern and suburban cities where gangs "are not an issue" and local officials and authorities are in denial.

And once MS-13 takes hold in a community, it grows fast. The gang reportedly has some 300 members in suburban Long Island. A few years back it didn't have any.

Once MS-13 shows up on the radar, some local officials and authorities will take action. In Nassau County, for example, a joint gang task force headed by the FBI and comprised of local police departments, has arrested 16 leaders of MS-13. They were charged with two murders, assault, conspiracy, and firearms violations.

Such investigations aren't easy because MS-13 has a pretty strident zero-tolerance policy toward anyone who informs the cops of their activities.

Court papers reveal that one of the Nassau County defendants was captured in a secretly recorded telephone conversation detailing how he killed a male victim because he had provided law enforcement officials with information and that he had "put one in his chest and three in the head." In another recorded conversation, a second defendant said he killed a young female because, in part, she had also provided information to law enforcement.

Law Enforcement Response

The senseless violence of MS-13 has shocked the local citizens of Nassau County, so the Nassau County Executive appointed a "gang czar" to deal with the increasing gang problem.

A seasoned, dedicated officer, the new "czar," in reality, will find it difficult to accomplish what he has been mandated to do. His department, like many across the nation, is at its lowest staffing levels in recent history, and he has been given no additional personnel or resources to combat the problem. The public was placated by the appointment, but while politicians put Band-Aids on deep cuts, the problem continues to escalate on Long Island.

And Long Island is not alone. Nationally, police departments are dealing with the surge in violence emanating from MS-13 members.

In Charlotte, N.C., 53 gang members were arrested as part of Operation Fed Up, which targeted MS-13 members. Officials in the medium-sized Southern city say MS-13 has been involved in at least 11 murders in the Charlotte area since 2000. And with a membership estimated at 200, MS-13 is by far Charlotte's largest gang.

Some 400 miles north of Charlotte, the northern Virginia and southern Maryland communities around Washington, D.C., have become MS-13 turf. Local authorities estimate that there are between 5,000 and 6,000 MS-13 members in the metropolitan area.

And where MS-13 goes, violence follows. In July 2003, an 18-year-old federal witness was stabbed to death; [in May 2004], a 16-year-old boy had his hands almost completely chopped off with a machete; and a week later a 17-year-old was shot and murdered. All three crimes were tied to MS-13 members.

The rapid increase in MS-13 activity along the corridor between Charlotte and D.C. is simply explained by Det. Tim Jolly, a gang specialist with the Charlotte-Mecklenburg Police Department. The area has the nation's second highest population of Salvadoran immigrants.

A Violent Threat

One of the more unusual aspects of MS-13 when compared to other street gangs is that it is extremely flexible in its activity. While some gangs are only into drugs, MS-13 will do any crime at any time. Sgt. George Norris, supervisor of the gang unit in the Prince George's County (Md.) Police Department, says MS-13 doesn't sling drugs in his jurisdiction. "We see mostly citizen robberies, auto theft, shootings and cuttings, and homicides," he says, adding that drug sales by MS-13 may be just a matter of time.

When MS-13 moves into a new community it tends to announce its presence with violence. The same can be true when a new leader takes over the local cliques.

Norris says gang members from other areas had once been able to join the new gang by simply being "jumped in." But now that new leaders have moved into Prince George's County and consolidated the cliques, the gang's local culture has become more violent and vicious.

"According to one of our informers, things have changed," says Norris. "Now in order to get your letters or clique [symbols] tattooed on you, you have to also put in some violent act to show your commitment."

U.S. officials from the MS-13 National Gang Task force meet with law-enforcement officials from El Salvador, Honduras, and Mexico to discuss the international criminal gang, also known as Mara Salvatrucha.

And MS-13 violence is not restricted to civilians, rival gang members, and clique traitors; the gang will go after cops. Threats against police officers, known to gang members as "green light" notices, have increased so much in the past few years that the Virginia Gang Association has warned officers in Virginia and states to the north and south [of it] to be wary of MS-13 members.

Charlotte-Mecklenburg's Jolly says he is aware of the threats against police officers in his community and in Virginia. Prince George's County's Norris says he's heard them, too. "If you do something to them, their natural response is, 'OK, I'm going to kill you,'" he says. "Or at least they talk like they will."

Norris dismisses some of MS-13's threats, but that doesn't mean that officers should take all MS-13 threats lightly. The gang is extremely violent and it has attacked and will continue to attack anyone who gets in its way. That includes law enforcement officers.

International Operations

Named for La Mara, a street in San Salvador, and the Salvatrucha guerillas who fought in El Salvador's bloody civil war, Mara Salvatrucha 13 was organized in Los Angeles in the late '80s. At first, the gang's primary purpose was to defend Salvadoran immigrants from being preyed upon by other L.A. street gangs.

But like any other street gang that was created to defend a particular ethnic group, MS-13 was quickly perverted until its primary purpose was preying upon the Salvadoran community. It also violently defends its turf against any other gang that might seek to slice away a piece of its action.

Gang members sometimes wear blue and white, colors taken from the national flag of El Salvador. They can also sport numerous body and even face tattoos. However, some members are much less visible and therefore much more dangerous.

Recent reports indicate that MS-13 has expanded from California to Alaska, Oregon, Utah, Texas, Nevada, Oklahoma, Illinois, Michigan, New York, Maryland, Virginia, Georgia, Washington, D.C., and Florida. The gang has also been exported back to Central America.

It's estimated that there are 36,000 MS-13 members in Honduras alone. In Honduras, according to a March 2004 report prepared by the Washington, D.C.-based, right-wing think tank the Maldon Institute, MS-13 has, with increasing frequency, resorted to leaving a dismembered corpse, complete with a decapitated head, as a calling card. Recently, according to the report, such a grisly message was left with a note for the Honduran president.

The note is supposed to have stated the gang's displeasure with an August 2003 law that made it illegal to be a part of a gang. Under Honduran law gang leaders can be sentenced to prison for up to 12 years and rank-and-file members from six to nine years, just for being in the gang. A gang member can be arrested for simply having a tattoo.

El Salvador has also launched a crackdown on MS-13. A police offensive called "Operation Strong-arm" has resulted in the arrest of more than 4,000 gang members.

Gangs Keep Moving and Growing

For MS-13, these are small losses. The gang is nothing if not mobile. When it feels heat in the U.S., it moves to another state. When it feels heat in El Salvador and Honduras, it sets up operations in Mexico.

The Maldon Institute report indicates that MS-13 "appears to be in control of much of the Mexican border and, in addition to its smuggling and contraband rackets, the gang collects money from illegal immigrants that it helps [move] across the border into the United States."

The ultra-conservative Maldon Institute is known for doomsday predictions when it comes to the U.S.-Mexico border. But there can be no denial that MS-13 is very active in smuggling people, drugs, and guns across the border. And independent reports indicate that many illegal immigrants have been assaulted, robbed, and even raped by MS-13 members.

Mexico is now taking steps to fight back against MS-13. In December, Mexican authorities arrested 224 gang members in response to what they called a threat to national security. Among the arrests were members of MS-13 who were charged with trafficking in drugs and firearms across Mexico and Central America.

While some of the Central American countries appear to be cracking down on MS-13, serious problems still exist. And they are being missed by politically correct reporters who want to tout U.S.-Latin American cooperation.

For example, on Long Island, the media was quick to cover an agreement between El Salvador and Suffolk County to share information on MS-13. What the local reporters didn't cover was a much more serious issue. If these gang members commit serious offenses, they can return home, and there is no extradition agreement. And, of course, they are doing so in increasing numbers.

"I would say that between Honduras and El Salvador, there are seven or eight people we are seeking to take into custody," says Lt. Dennis Farrell, head homicide investigator for the Nassau County Police Department. "Proportionally, if you take that across the country, the numbers are astronomical, the number of people who have probably fled to these two countries."

Farrell says that two gang members who his detectives are looking to arrest for two separate murders are now living in the same town in El Salvador. He calls the situation extremely frustrating. "You undertake a very in-depth and comprehensive investigation, pursue all possible leads, build a case, essentially conduct a successful investigation, only to have it thwarted by the fact that after having identified the killer or killers, you are unable, under the present international agreements, to return them to Nassau County to face murder charges.

"Even more than that frustration, how about the injustice and sense of desperation on the part of families who have lost loved ones? where is the measure of justice? There is really no justice for those families, and absent some reworked or new initiative between our state department and those sovereign states, I don't see any change m this condition in the foreseeable future," Farrell adds.

Stronger Laws Are Needed

In addition to extradition treaties, many gang investigators believe stricter and more uniform laws are needed here in this country. According to Charlotte-Mecklenburg's Jolly, one of the reasons MS-13 has migrated to the East Coast is the strict anti-gang laws on the West Coast. He also believes that, with the stricter gang laws in Central America, many MS-13 members may be coming back to the United States illegally.

With the number of MS-13 members growing nationwide (some cliques now even accept non-Hispanic members), and the violence escalating, the future for law enforcement appears grim.

"They adapt to what the police do," says Prince George's County's Norris. "They will change the way they operate, depending on the way things are enforced by the police. If there is no enforcement, they will wear their colors and bandanas because in the communities they are in it is common knowledge and the people fear them, so it is a form of intimidation.

"Once the police recognize and confront them, they will change and wear different colors from the blue and white, no bandana on their head, maybe now in their pocket, and instead of the number 13 they will wear 67 or 76 because it equals 13. They adapt so it is a continually evolving thing."

While the nation focuses on terrorism, the issue of gang violence has taken a lower priority. But to many, the violent acts of M-13 members are more of an everyday threat that is being overlooked.

TEN

Gang Intervention Programs Are Successful

Victor M. Gonzalez Jr.

> Gangs are a problem in many communities and threaten especially preschool- and school-age children, who are often at risk of gang involvement, argues Victor M. Gonzalez Jr. in the following viewpoint. Gang intervention, prevention, and suppression programs are successful when communities work together against gang activity, he asserts. Successful intervention programs monitor gangs while reaching out to children and families in the community with services designed to reduce gang involvement and the impact of gangs, Gonzalez contends. Focusing on keeping children in school is an important aspect of a successful gang intervention program, the author maintains.
>
> Victor M. Gonzalez Jr. is the director of program services for the Mayor's Anti-Gang Office in Houston, Texas. He has more than twenty years of experience in gang outreach and family services working with juvenile delinquents.

[The Houston, Texas, Mayor's Anti-Gang Office] has developed many truancy pilot projects; we have learned that a combination of early interventions, family involvement, cooperation with the court, and frequent referrals to outside services are essential to a successful program. We have also learned that when

Victor M. Gonzalez Jr., from *The Truancy and Gang Connection: Reflections from the Mayor's Anti-Gang Office, Houston, TX*, National Center for School Engagement, 2006. Reproduced by permission.

schools take proactive measures and police become involved, much good work can be done to curb truancy. This essay is intended to provide a better understanding of how gang involvement, family dysfunction and drug use combine to create school attendance problems. It is important to recognize the early signs of trouble and to develop proactive interventions. Empowering youth and families to do better is a critical part of this process; it takes their work as well to prevent truancy.

Gangs and Preschool Children

When gangs are part of a community, children are exposed early to drug use, violence, and other negative influences. This early exposure can be detrimental to the life of a young person. Even preschool age children, four and five years old, are exposed to many negative things in their environment when gangs are present, putting them at a higher risk for gang involvement themselves.

Communities with large numbers of dysfunctional families often have high rates of gang activity. Parents who have poor communication skills, past gang involvement, poor parenting skills, domestic violence issues and/or drug problems contribute to the challenges of very young children. This ultimately makes it difficult for young children to get a good start in school. In addition, when families do not value the importance of an education, commitment to school may not be emphasized. Also, when parents have limited educational attainment, children are often not prepared for school.

Children from problematic families develop inappropriate behavior before they even get to school. It is common for these children to be physically and verbally aggressive towards other students because of poor role modeling in their communities or families. Ill-prepared students do not enjoy their school experience and have school related problems early in life. Early on, children exposed to gang-related activity in the home have difficulty understanding structure in the classroom. Teachers typically try to redirect problem behavior, but these interventions can be perceived so negatively by these children that they can develop an intense dislike for teachers and the school environment. Ultimately, children do not want to return to the classroom.

Gangs in Elementary School

Addressing gang behavior in elementary school is crucial to preventing gang involvement. If there is a gang presence in elementary and middle school, aggressive behavior or delayed learning can become more ingrained. At-risk children are sometimes made fun of due to their disciplinary problems. This spurs additional aggressive behavior toward fellow students. The combination of feeling unaccepted by students, teachers and principals leads to school disengagement and the need to seek a group that will accept them. Hence, affiliation with a gang can help meet their needs. In some cases, students do not actively seek out gang affiliation but are bullied into the lifestyle. Some are recruited or sought after in elementary school by older members to continue to build the numbers in the gang.

The gang lifestyle creates a mindset of loyalty, pride and love for young students who are disengaged from school. When bonds are created among gang members, gangs replace school and family. A child will do whatever his/her new friends want him/her to do. The pressure to join the gang officially becomes impossible to resist. The initiation process has life altering implications. New gang members follow all rules provided by the gang and feel obligated to do everything with the gang. This bond is extremely difficult to break, and is a major obstacle re-engaging students in school.

Middle School Gang Activity

The transition to middle school from elementary school brings its own set of social problems. Many students in sixth grade who do not have healthy self-esteem and do not feel they are a part of the school will continue to associate with the gang and consider initiation. They will experiment with gang-related behavior, such as graffiti, fighting, bullying, gang dress, gang talk and practicing gang hand signs. Drive-bys, guns, drug usage, sex, and violence will become part of life for this young person. Gangs meet regularly, and gang activity occurs daily. When a student decides to join a gang, academics cease to be important. School becomes the last thing on a young gang member's mind.

If a middle school gang member considers trying to re-engage in school, it is likely the aspiration will be short lived. Once he/she falls far behind academically, it becomes clear to the gang member that it is too late and there is no need to attend school at all. However, it is not uncommon to meet students who are 16 and in the eight grade who are still trying to pass and get to high school. Nevertheless, many will seek dropping out, but fear truancy laws and court fines. The court process can be beneficial, especially in the sixth grade, given the student's ignorance of the municipal court system. Early intervention is recommended at this point to deter further truancy.

Impact of Gangs in High School

The transition to high school can be difficult if a student gets involved in a gang during ninth grade. School attendance is the first thing affected by gang membership. Many students between the ages of 14 and 16 increase their gang activity as they attempt to create a name for themselves within the gang, on the streets, and with the rival gangs. It is not uncommon for gang members to skip classes yet remain on school grounds. Dedicated gang members are expected to actively recruit, fight or sell drugs on campus as much as possible.

Many gang members meet before school to get high and discuss campus gang activity. After using drugs in the morning, many decide to skip classes and just "hang out" all day, which increases the number of days they miss school. Sometimes gang members will not go to school if rivals are present. Eventually skipping school becomes a habit. Absences lead to disengagement from school, which whittles away the motivation to complete school assignments. The combination of poor attendance and incomplete homework ensures failing grades and retention. The prospect of high school graduation fades with every "F" a student receives.

Even if gang members do not fail their classes, school administrators tolerate gang members only minimally. When school staff cannot understand or deal effectively with the gang mentality, they apply zero tolerance rules and quickly expel most active gang members.

Baton Rouge, Louisiana: Operation Eiger

Average Number of New Violent Offenses

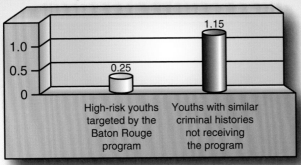

Philadelphia, Pennsylvania: Alive at 25

Youth Homicide Rate per Year (ages 7–24) in the 25th District

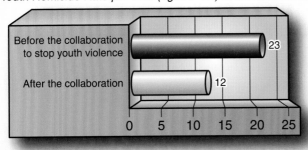

Boston, Massachusetts: Operation Ceasefire

Average Monthly Homicides

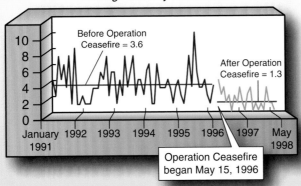

Taken from: *Caught in the Crossfire: Arresting Gangs by Investing in Kids*, Fight Crime, Invest in Kids, 2004.

Gang activity affects non-members as well. Many students will not want to go to school if fights occur regularly on campus and if getting to school is too dangerous.

Challenges of Gang Intervention

Challenges to working with gang members include:

- gang mentality
- lack of student motivation
- school staff labeling gang members as "bad kids"
- weak truancy laws
- lack of consistency in enforcing attendance policies
- insufficient school staff to monitor attendance

With the rise in gang involvement in Houston, and throughout the country, it is important to remember a lot of work remains to be done to address this issue appropriately. Many approaches and strategies have been discussed nationally. However, stakeholders need to dedicate themselves and their services to helping this population succeed in life. We must address the problem of gangs through prevention, intervention and suppression. It will take a collaboration of stakeholders such as social services, schools, businesses, law enforcement, and criminal justice to come together to make an impact on gangs.

School attendance personnel, social workers, school administrators, police, the juvenile court, and community members including businesses must collaborate to address truancy and tackle these challenges.

Components of a Successful Intervention Program

- *School attendance personnel* need to examine the way attendance is tracked and monitored in order to have an accurate count of days or classes missed.
- *Social workers* need to follow up with students who are just beginning to skip school as well as those who have an excessive number of absences. The longer truancy is not addressed, the more problematic it becomes for both the school and the

student. There are many reasons for truancy, and they need to be explored and assessed in order to determine what methods will be effective in re-engaging students.

- *School administrators* need to ensure that there is a mechanism to help students who need differentiated services no matter how severe their attendance problems. Although gang members create the conditions that cause schools to push them out, alternative educational options need to be available for them.
- *Police* should be visible and bring truants back to school. Officers can either dedicate time during the day, or funds can be dedicated for over-time pay, to make home visits to provide warnings and serve citations to parents of truants.
- *The court* can provide creative sanctions, instead of just imposing fines. Many families of truants have issues that have gone unaddressed for long periods of time. The leverage of a judge can help get these families appropriate services.

First Lady Laura Bush shakes hands with a representative of Cease Fire Chicago, while a client of the program looks on. Mrs. Bush visited Cease Fire as part of her campaign to get kids out of gangs and back in school.

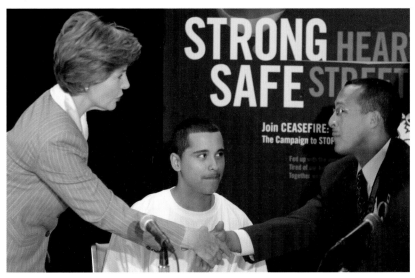

- *All stakeholders* can work cooperatively to launch truancy awareness campaigns that involve distributing literature and prominently posting truancy and curfew laws. Taking the time to educate students, families, and communities about truancy laws is very important to increasing school attendance.
- *Business owners* must ensure that they do not serve or employ school-aged youth during the school day.

The Importance of Gang Assessments

Gang members are harder to help than students who are truant for other reasons. They need specific attention focused on employment, counseling, tattoo removal and educational choices. While success may be limited, depending on the level of gang involvement, attempts to intervene are important because even gang members sometimes try to return to school.

We in the Mayor's Anti-Gang Office have learned from our work with gangs and truants that without information and resources, it is hard to provide the services that our community needs to help gang impacted areas. Conducting assessments is important to determine a base from which to work. Assessments identify a set of problems and set the stage for the kind of difficult discussions necessary to developing cooperative strategies that impact the whole community.

Gangs are a cancer that can take over a community quickly. Therefore, gang activity must be monitored regularly; ignoring gang issues is extremely costly both financially and socially. It creates an unsafe and miserable atmosphere for families. Families who feel there is no hope for any improvement will not be motivated to do what is necessary to raise their children to stay in school or avoid gangs.

Successful Gang Intervetion: Houston, TX

The Mayor's Anti-Gang Office currently operates two gang intervention programs. The Gang Reduction Team is responsible for citywide outreach to gang involved youth and is comprised of six members. The team specifically targets 13- to 24-year-old gang-involved youth from Houston's most active and dangerous gangs. The Gang Free Schools Project is a three-person team that targets Houston's east end. This comprehensive model is designed to reduce gang violence by engaging community stakeholders, police, criminal justice, schools and gang outreach workers. The model works on five principles: suppression, opportunities provision, community mobilization, social intervention and organizational development and change.

The intervention services both teams offer include:

- Outreach and response to gang involved individuals and those at risk of gang involvement by intervention specialists to provide case management, counseling, mediation, mentoring, and encouragement of lawful use of the criminal justice system.
- Referrals to drug counseling, tattoo removal, job readiness programs, and/or placement in alternative educational programs.
- Gang Incident Response to reduce gang violence in the community, schools and facilities where gang members are present. Mediations are conducted to assist this process.
- Operation of parenting support groups, counseling, and family intervention sessions for the parents of gang involved youth.
- Educational instruction and social skill building targeted at gang involved and at-risk youth.
- Distribution of gang awareness and prevention materials to youth, parents, educators, and the general public during public presentations on gang awareness, intervention and prevention.

Together, these two teams have made an impact in educating the Houston community about dealing with gangs. As a result of their interventions, the teams have helped reduce gang related incidents among some of the most active gang members in Houston.

ELEVEN

Gang Intervention Programs Are Not Successful

Hector Gonzalez

> Most gang prevention and intervention programs use a similar approach in which a former gang member lectures young people on the dangers of being in a gang, states Hector Gonzalez in the following viewpoint. These programs expect young people to make changes in their lives based on the experiences of another person, usually a stranger, he points out. Young people will only change their behavior after reflection on their own lives, goals, and dreams, he maintains. Instead of standard gang intervention programs, young people need opportunities for self-evaluation and self-knowledge, Gonzalez concludes.
>
> Hector Gonzalez is an independent writer, commentator, and anti-gang youth mentor. He has been a regular contributor to the Pacific News Service, *Silicon Valley Debug,* and numerous Web publications.

I attended a "gang intervention" workshop a few days back. Being that I work with young gang members myself I wanted to see how other people were approaching their work. A Latino male with tattoos addressed the classroom about gangs. It reminded me of when I was 13, when I was the youth listening to the Latino

Hector Gonzalez, "Never Have and Never Will: Why Gang Intervention Programs Don't Work," *De-Bug,* August 16, 2005. Reproduced by permission.

male with tattoos give his spiel about why gangs are bad. The program was a repetitive discussion that went around in circles.

The programs both then and now consisted of a Latino male with a beard that lectured why people joined gangs and the results of gang banging. They show pictures of dead gang members, pictures of gang tattoos, they talked about prison life, and then gave a compelling story of how they changed their lives. What I have come to realize is that people don't change by reflecting on the lives of others, they change by reflecting on themselves.

At the age of 18, not too long after I had graduated high school, I was offered a position as a tutor for an organization called Filipino Youth Coalition. One month into my job, one

A man who has spent one third of his life behind prison walls speaks to youth offenders at the Livingston County Jail in Howell, Michigan. Some argue that programs like these that try to scare kids into good behavior are unlikely to work.

of my co-workers gave up his position as a Youth Mentor/Gang Intervention Specialist and the position was offered to me. When I first began, I was lost—a young adult that gave lectures to kids from a curriculum that even I found boring. I realized that if there was anything that was profound, it wasn't in the workbooks, but in the relationship that I was building with the students.

Ever since that first job, I have worked in the middle schools throughout the East Side of San Jose [California]. When I returned for my second year of the program, one of the students from the prior year came to the after school program and told me that she wanted to come in but that she was now in a foster home and that she would have to ask her social worker to let her stay after school. I walked with the student to the front of the school to talk to her social worker, and she explained to me that it was part of her foster home's policy to be home by a certain time, and that participating in an after school program wouldn't allow her to come home on time. As these words came out of her mouth, tears began flowing down the student's cheeks. I understood my job in a much different form after this point. I realized that people's testimonies of [their] lives were much more profound [than] any lecture I could ever give.

Rethinking Gang Intervention

Many times, people that do gang intervention say that people join gangs because they want belonging or because they want to fill a void. If that's the case, then young people should be given the opportunity to reflect on those voids and lack of belongingness as opposed to having a discussion on how "gangs are not the answer." Besides, the only person that would know that is the person who feels empty and like they don't belong to anything.

The Filipino Youth Coalition (FYC) gave me the opportunity to develop my own curriculum. The truth of the matter is that although I developed a curriculum, I didn't even follow it usually. Most of the times the young people were the ones that lead the direction of the program, guiding the discussion of what they felt and told me [their] life stories. I touched the general topics that the program and school required me to touch, such as drug prevention,

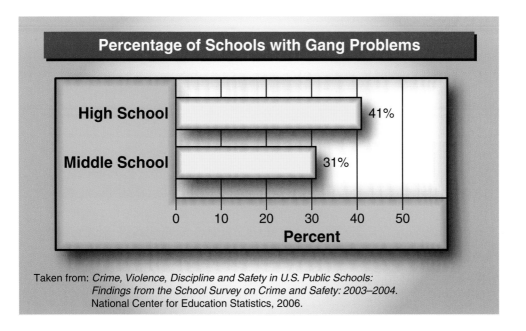

Percentage of Schools with Gang Problems

High School — 41%

Middle School — 31%

Percent

Taken from: *Crime, Violence, Discipline and Safety in U.S. Public Schools: Findings from the School Survey on Crime and Safety: 2003–2004.* National Center for Education Statistics, 2006.

peers, identity, family and academics. I would run my program by creating a space where the students had an opportunity to identify themselves before I could identify them. This was in some ways the opposite of the rest of the spaces they entered. Every other group, or institution that they belonged to identified them first. The school gave them an identity, they were either good or bad students, their teachers identified them as being trouble-makers, disruptive, and as low-performing students. I asked them to tell me who they were, and they described themselves as strong young people, loyal to their family and friends, and they had dreams and goals.

[Since 2001], I have devoted a good portion of my life working with youth throughout [San Jose's East Side]. Some of the most profound stories that I have ever heard have come from young people close to a decade younger than I am. During a workshop with about 20 young people in a room and me as the only adult, a 13-year-old female shared the testimony of her life. She told the classroom that her health is dictated by her mother's drug problem, for when her mother was pregnant her mother abused methamphetamines. Her mother died not too long ago from an overdose. Her reflecting on this event is much stronger than any lecture I could ever give to her.

Although most of my work took place at the schools, it continued in the streets. I did home visits in hoods such as A-town, Poco Way, and Verde to name a few. I hung out with them, met their OG's [old gangsters], congregated as if I was one of their own. The last time I went to A-town, I drove by and parked my car in front of around 20 Cambodian youth. Most were between 13–17 years of age, all in blue, one guy was holding a Beebee gun, a couple of them were smoking cigarettes, I approached my little homie Peter. He shook my hand as his homie was riding his lowrider bike, the one I bought him for keeping his grades up and graduating eighth grade. Peter's older brother is currently locked up, and both Peter and his little sister recently completed their probation hours. His lips are very dark and he has scars on his face, his knuckles have scars on them as well, and he wears a tank top to display his homemade tattoo that spells out his name. I looked at his community. A-town stands for Avalani Town. Avalani is a street that contains apartments mostly occupied with Cambodian folks. In this particular visit to A-town I observed everything that my eyes captured; the kids running on the streets, all the A-town Crips lined up on the sidewalk, cars with busted tires, and apartment lawns with no grass, decorated by scattered liquor bottles. No matter how awful anyone thinks A-town is, it belongs to Peter, it is his, and he takes pride in it. Peter lives gang culture, he doesn't need anyone to define it for him or tell him the consequences of gang banging; his family is living it. If Peter ever does decide to leave his gang, it would be through a realization that will manifest through analyzing his life and through self-discovery.

The Role of Mentors

I realized that my role as a mentor was to provide a space for self-discovery; there is no setting better than a youth retreat outside of their hoods. [In July 2005], along with some colleagues, I took 14 youth camping, three of them were females and the rest were males. They were all eighth graders going into high school. They came from all gang backgrounds, Norteno, Sureno, Cambodian and Laotian Crips. Half of the kids had criminal records, and most of them had been involved in a gang-related fight at their school. Some of them had tattoos, and all of them claimed to have a gang affiliation.

During the first day of the three-day camp I asked them to introduce themselves by answering, "What is it that you fear?" With the exception of two kids, they all said that they feared their fathers. For the first time, they all shared an intimate moment with their "enemies." Throughout the camp we did activities that talked about our own strengths, families, and other discussion that dealt with us taking control of our destinies. For those three days they bonded; they played hide and seek together, ate together, laughed together, and shed tears together. The last night young Crips, Surenos, and Nortenos hugged one another.

Although they returned to their hoods represented by different gang sets, they will embrace the moment when with the help of rival gang members, they were able to share some of the most symbolic moments of [their] lives, reflect on them, and heal their wounds.

After hearing the testimonies of so many kids, I know for a fact that the only way to help anyone transform [his or her] life is by creating a space where people can have intimate moments by sharing [their] lives, reflecting on them, and finding the solution for [their] problems by themselves and for themselves.

TWELVE

Community-Based Gang Intervention Is Effective

Phelan Wyrick

> Gang activity and neighborhood violence can be reduced if young people are prevented from joining gangs, argues Phelan Wyrick in the following viewpoint. Community gang intervention programs can be developed to offer attractive alternatives to gang life, he contends. Effective antigang programs, he maintains, are those that address the needs that young people are trying to meet through gang membership, such as a sense of worth and belonging, improved self-esteem, and monetary gain. Successful community programs are partnerships that include social activities, employment opportunities, and ongoing support for youth at risk of gang involvement, Wyrick concludes.
>
> Phelan Wyrick is the gang program coordinator for the Demonstration Programs Division of the U.S. Department of Justice's Office of Juvenile Justice and Delinquency Prevention. He is affiliated with various initiatives, including the federal Gang Reduction Program, the Gang-Free Schools and Communities Program, and the National Youth Gang Center.

Gang prevention is an effort to change the life trajectory of a young person who is otherwise likely to join a gang. Young

Phelan Wyrick, "Gang Prevention: How to Make the 'Front End' of Your Anti-Gang Effort Work," *United States Attorneys' Bulletin*, vol. 54, no. 3, May 2006, pp. 53-57, 60.

people who join gangs are exercising a choice. The decision to join a gang is usually not made under extreme duress, though there are pressures placed on adolescents in this area. In fact, young people frequently see gangs as an attractive choice or a solution to their problems. From a practical perspective, gang prevention must address the needs and desires that underlie these choices in order to be effective. There are several sources of information on what young people want and what they need that have direct relevance to gang prevention. The first source of information on this topic comes from what we know about normal adolescent development.

Adolescents and Gangs

It is not a coincidence that the onset of adolescence overlaps with the average age for joining a gang (twelve to fourteen years old). The central developmental challenge of adolescence is described by psychologist Erik Erickson as "identity vs. role confusion." In short, all adolescents are trying to figure out who they are as they move toward adulthood. It is not uncommon for them to "try on" different identities during this time. This is a normal process that is harmless for most youth, but can also lead to risky and illegal behaviors.

The heightened importance of peer groups, and what psychologists call "egocentrism," are two other key developmental characteristics of adolescence. As children turn into adolescents, their focus of social attention and approval shifts from adults to their peers. During this time, adolescents become increasingly egocentric—meaning that they perceive the world as revolving around them—and they are deficient in the ability to accept other perspectives.

Egocentrism has a number of consequences. For example, otherwise neutral events are more likely seen as personal slights, perceived injustices are often blown out of proportion, and the ability to empathize with others is underdeveloped. Taken together and applied in the context of a community with high levels of gang activity, normal adolescent development can result in very dangerous outcomes. Consider the common adolescent experience of being embarrassed or humiliated in front of a group of peers. This situation is difficult for any adolescent, but it can become deadly in the context of gang involvement. Gangs have access to illegal guns and norms that support violence as an appropriate method for resolving conflict. Many in local law enforcement are well aware of how frequently gang violence stems from seemingly minor "beefs" between adolescents.

Being Pulled into a Gang

Gang researchers Scott Decker and Barrik Van Winkle describe forces that "pull" and "push" young people into gangs. If you ask current or former gang members, they are likely to describe the "pulls." That is, they will describe those attractive features of gang membership and the gang lifestyle that typically include respect, excitement, social opportunities, protection, and money.

Respect in the context of gang membership translate more directly into intimidation or fear. Everyone wishes to be treated with respect, but gang membership offers young people a shortcut to earning respect. Excitement in the gang refers to risky behaviors, illegal activity, and generally upending the societal norms that define appropriate and inappropriate behavior, for example, parties where alcohol, drugs, and members of the opposite sex are readily available.

The desire for protection among young people sometimes strikes a chord of compassion in adults. Some are tempted to ask, "Could it be that young people are really safer in gangs?" The answer is no. Despite myths to the contrary, gangs do not protect their members. Gang members are more likely to become victims because they embrace a lifestyle in which their own violence begets more violence.

Finally, although some gangs and gang members make large sums of money through drug distribution or other criminal enterprises, many gangs lack the organizational sophistication to carry out these operations and, those that do, tend to concentrate most of the profits in the hands of a few people at the top. Thus, gang members often suggest motivations for joining gangs that seem like rational needs and desires. Gangs do not deliver on these promises, however, and the fun and excitement that are delivered lead to hazardous and destructive behaviors that can be fatal or life altering.

Being Pushed into a Gang

The forces that "push" young people into gangs have been verified by numerous longitudinal research studies that examine the conditions early in life that are related to an increased probability of gang membership in later years. Researchers have identified dozens of these conditions, called risk factors, that fall into five general categories or life domains. Researchers James "Buddy" Howell and Arlen Egley of the National Youth Gang Center (NYGC) summarized the five domains of risk factors for gang membership:

- Community or neighborhood risk factors—such as access to drugs, availability of illegal firearms, and the local crime rate.
- Family risk factors—such as sibling antisocial behavior, low parental control, and family poverty.
- School risk factors—such as low academic aspirations, low school attachment, and learning disabilities.
- Peer group risk factors—such as association with delinquent peers and/or aggressive peers.
- Individual risk factors—such as aggression or fighting, conduct disorders, and antisocial beliefs.

The more risk factors in the life of a young person, the greater the probability for joining a gang. A study of Seattle youth found that those with seven or more risk factors at age ten to twelve were thirteen times more likely to join a gang than those with no risk factors. This cumulative effect of risk factors is very important to gang prevention and intervention. No one risk factor rises clearly above the rest, and different configurations of risk factors are likely to be present in different communities and for different individuals. Thus, gang prevention and intervention efforts must be poised to identify those risk factors that are at play, determine which are most amenable to change, and target those with effective services at the community, family, or individual level.

Effective Gang Prevention

In summary, there are a variety of things that young people want and need that have direct relevance to gang prevention. Adolescents need opportunities to explore their identity and the healthy paths to adulthood. They need to do this with their peers in a social setting that is safe. They want to have fun and excitement. They want to be respected. They want access to money. Indeed, many who work with and have studied at-risk

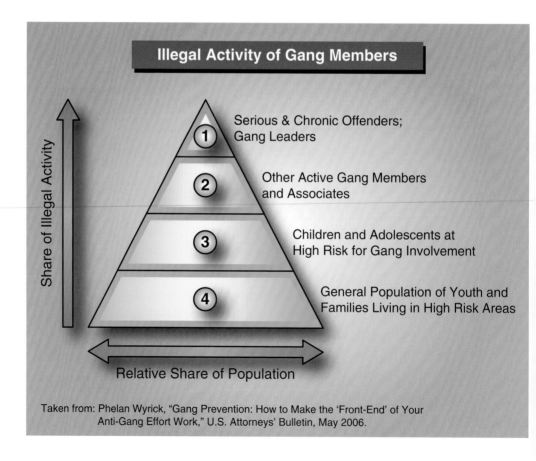

Taken from: Phelan Wyrick, "Gang Prevention: How to Make the 'Front-End' of Your Anti-Gang Effort Work," U.S. Attorneys' Bulletin, May 2006.

youth find that they would be content simply to have improved access to meaningful employment. They have a wide variety of needs and personal challenges that fall into the five risk-factor domains related to their community, school, family, peers, and personal issues.

The needs and desires of youth can point the way to alternatives that can compete with the features of gangs that attract them. These needs and desires also help us understand what is required for effective support systems. Superior gang prevention efforts blend effective support systems with attractive alternatives to gangs, and target these services to adolescents who are most at risk for gang involvement.

Community-Based Gang Prevention

It is frequently said that no two gangs are alike. Even gangs that share the same name may have very different structures, group dynamics, membership characteristics, and offending patterns. Likewise, no two communities are exactly alike, as local leaders and community members are quick to point out. The best anti-gang initiatives are tailored to meet local needs and challenges, but benefit from broader-based research and best practices. On the front end of these initiatives are concerted efforts to understand how local gang characteristics and dynamics interact with a range of social forces that are also local and community-based (for example, demographic trends, housing, employment, historical events, law enforcement practices, and others). Before tackling the local issues, there is value in considering a general framework for the ways that gangs affect communities.

Gang Member Activity

[The diagram "Illegal Activity of Gang Members] . . . provides a general sense of how gangs relate to illegal activity and population in a community with gang problems. Group 1, at the top of the triangle, represents serious, chronic, and violent offenders that are a relatively small portion of the population, but are responsible for a disproportionately large share of illegal activity. Group 2 consists of gang-involved youth and associates who make up a relatively larger share of the population, are responsible for significant levels of illegal activity, but are not necessarily in the highest offending category. Members of this group typically range in age from twelve to twenty-four years. Group 3 is made up of the seven- to fourteen-year-old youth who have already displayed early signs of delinquency and risk for gang membership, but are not yet gang-involved. They will not all go into gangs, but they are the likely pool of candidates for gang membership in the near future. Group 4 represents everyone else living in a community where gangs are present.

These four groups clearly relate to four basic strategies for combating gangs. Members of Group 1 are candidates for targeted enforcement and prosecution because of their high level of involvement in crime and the low probability that other strategies will reduce their criminal behavior. Effective enforcement and prosecution targeted at this small group of individuals will reduce community crime because each individual in this group is responsible for committing a large number of crimes. These individuals represent perhaps as little as 7 or 8 percent of offenders, but may account for 40 or 50 percent of all crime. Members of Group 2 are candidates for gang intervention, members of Group 3 are candidates for secondary prevention, and members of Group 4 are recipients of primary prevention services. . . .

Community-Based Gang Intervention

Gang intervention includes a balance of services and opportunities with supervision and accountability (namely, "carrot and stick") that is tailored to the circumstances of individual gang-involved or high-risk youth. Gang members and associates typically engage in elevated levels of violence, property crimes, weapons violations, and drug offenses relative to their nongang-involved peers. They are also more likely to be exposed to numerous risk factors in the five domains already discussed. Beyond that, there are few simple ways to characterize them.

- They may or may not be in school.
- They may or may not be employed.
- They may or may not be on probation or otherwise in the juvenile or criminal justice system.

Effective gang intervention requires coordinated partnerships of agencies and service providers that use information-sharing across agency types (police, juvenile courts, schools, prosecution, community agencies) to facilitate targeting and outreach to gang-involved youth and their families, a system of graduated sanctions, and effective case management. Partners in gang intervention often include law enforcement, courts, probation offices, social services, employment services, schools, community groups, faith-based groups, and others.

The basic intervention message to gang-involved youth can be summed up as follows: "We are working together to reduce violence and gang activity in our community. We are aware of your gang involvement and are concerned about illegal activities and the safety threat you pose to yourself and others. We are offering alternatives to the gang lifestyle in the form of social services, job opportunities, and educational opportunities. Whether you pursue these alternatives or not, you will be held accountable if you continue to pose a threat to community safety."

Programs for At-Risk Youth

Secondary prevention refers to programs and services that are directed toward youth who have already displayed early signs of problem behavior and are at high-risk for gang involvement. This is the group that rises to the top of the prevention priority list for many people because they are most likely to face the choice of whether or not to join the gang in the near future. This is the group that most needs the three basic elements of effective gang prevention.

Former gang member Miguel Ramos works for Homeboy Industries, a non-profit organization that offers jobs to those who are looking to escape from gang life.

- Attractive alternatives. Attractive alternatives divert time and attention from the gang lifestyle by providing healthy and accessible venues for fun, excitement, and social interaction. These are safe venues to learn and practice healthy forms of gaining and showing respect.
- Effective support systems. Effective support systems are necessary to address specific social, emotional, and psychological needs and challenges faced by adolescents in general, and high-risk adolescents in particular.
- Accountability. Accountability is required to demonstrate and enforce clear expectations for appropriate behavior. Inappropriate behaviors in the context of prevention programs frequently do not rise to the level of illegal activity. Consequently, enforcing clear standards may take the form of withholding access to the most attractive features of program

participation. In cases where behaviors are more serious, clear and appropriate sanctions beyond the program should be readily available.

Programs for the Whole Community

Primary prevention refers to services and supports that reach the entire population in communities with high crime or gang activity. These efforts typically address needs or risk factors in a way that is available to all youth and families, or supports the community as a whole. Delivery of these services may flow through units of government, local schools, community organizations, or faith-based organizations.

Examples include public awareness campaigns, one-stop centers that improve access to public services, school-based life skills programs, community clean up and lighting projects, and community organizing. Such a broad range of activities does not strike some people as having much bearing on gang prevention but, in fact, gangs thrive in areas that appear to be forgotten or overlooked. When there is clear evidence that residents care about their community, gangs begin to lose their foothold. . . .

The most convincing advocates for the importance of gang prevention are the law enforcement officers and prosecutors who have worked for years arresting gang members. They are so convincing because they can give first-hand accounts of the young people that cycle into the gang lifestyle, become offenders, and become victims. Some die young, some go to prison, and some continue on a ruinous path into adulthood. Soon, their children are old enough to be next in line and the pattern continues. The goal of gang prevention is to interrupt this cycle. Some have viewed this as nothing more than a dream. Others are working hard to make it a reality. Whether that goal is achieved, or not, will depend on the willingness to dedicate time and money to this purpose in a way that will continue to build knowledge and increase the number and quality of gang prevention tools at a community's disposal.

THIRTEEN

Mentoring Is the Most Effective Gang Intervention

Thomas J. Smith

> Public programs that support at-risk youth normally focus on young children while offering limited, if any, services for adolescents, contends Thomas J. Smith. Research indicates that the most successful programs for at-risk teens rely on the involvement of adult mentors, he asserts. Adults who are committed to the mentoring relationship can have tremendous positive impact on young people, Smith argues, noting that at-risk youth in mentoring relationships tend to stay in school and to avoid involvement with drugs and violence.
>
> Thomas J. Smith has been a researcher and analyst with Public/Private Ventures, a national nonprofit organization dedicated to improving the effectiveness of social programs for youth and young adults. He has authored and contributed to numerous publications and research reports.

A variety of public systems and programs exist to meet the special needs of the nation's young people. Foster care, welfare, public health and juvenile justice are established, generally stable systems with a dependable source of funding, reflecting the nation's basic commitment to the well-being of children.

Thomas J. Smith, "Guides for the Journey: Supporting High-Risk Youth with Paid Mentors and Counselors," *Public/Private Ventures Briefs*, June 2004, pp. 5-7. Reproduced by permission.

To a considerable degree, these systems are protective and custodial. Their major focus is younger children, and (with the exception of juvenile justice) they offer a far more limited amount of support and services to adolescents and young adults. Indeed, outside of schools, "adolescent" programs in most communities are piecemeal mixes of public resources and private/nonprofit organizations—the second-chance network. Public funding for the network is scattered and undependable (except, again, for justice programs), and the offerings vary widely in their aims and quality.

Will Dunn is a former gang member—with a conviction for gun posession—who now mentors youth in Boston and tries to help them avoid the mistakes he made.

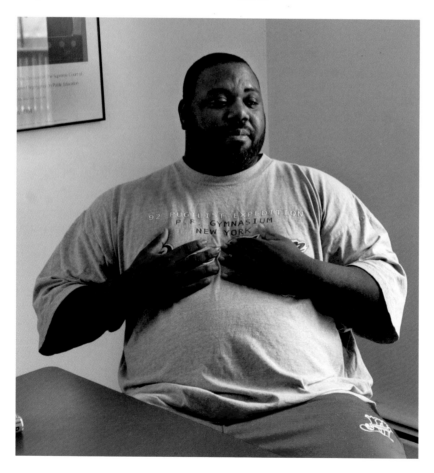

Adolescents Need Support Services

In part, this reflects a general societal belief that while young children may sometimes require special public intervention and protection, adolescents do not and are, in fact, quite adequately served by attendance in school. Unlike education or protective children's services, whose necessity and value are accepted, there is little public enthusiasm for extensive support systems for adolescents. The services that do exist have a strong local and voluntary flavor, depending as much or more on United Ways and local philanthropies as they do on public sources for support. Boys and Girls Clubs, Big Brothers Big Sisters and a range of community organizations (such as the Police Athletic League) are the mainstay of the network.

These programs mostly emphasize recreation, education and jobs. The federal Workforce Investment Act (WIA), which funds employment-related programming, is among the few flexible sources of support for adolescent nonschool programs (though much of it actually is spent on programming for youth in school). And while WIA funding does target low-income youth, most of the programming is of short duration and not always concentrated on youth who are most seriously at risk.

Given the fragmented nature of these services, young people, especially those at serious risk, are all too likely to fall through the cracks. The network is under-funded, unsophisticated and unconnected. It has little capacity for keeping track of youngsters once they leave a program, and adolescents are a mobile and volatile group, complicating matters further. The larger issue is this: Even when "high-risk" adolescents are identified, few services are available to assist them, and fewer still can assist them for an extended period.

Adult Mentors Can Make a Difference

Designing programs for young people is always likely to be as much a creative as a scientific process. Even granting that, more than two decades of research and evaluation have identified some basic principles that underpin successful programs and initiatives for

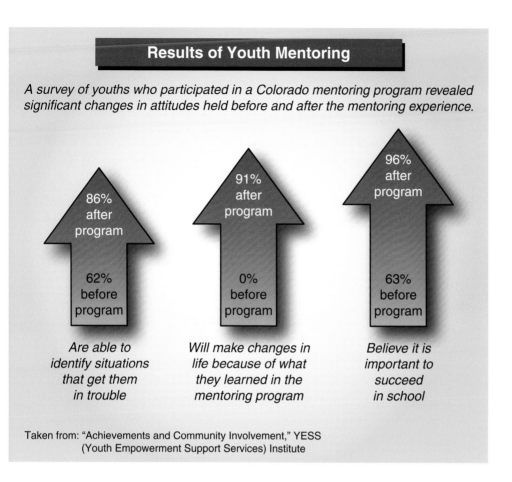

Results of Youth Mentoring

A survey of youths who participated in a Colorado mentoring program revealed significant changes in attitudes held before and after the mentoring experience.

86%
after
program

62%
before
program

Are able to
identify situations
that get them
in trouble

91%
after
program

0%
before
program

Will make changes in
life because of what
they learned in the
mentoring program

96%
after
program

63%
before
program

Believe it is
important to
succeed
in school

Taken from: "Achievements and Community Involvement," YESS
(Youth Empowerment Support Services) Institute

youth. One on which both research and common sense strongly agree is that the presence of caring and committed adults can make a strong difference in young people's lives.

Plentiful anecdotal evidence attests to the enormous positive impact adults can have. Stories of teachers, neighbors, local store owners and coaches who connect with a youngster are a staple in the youth field. And the work of scholars such as Emmy Werner has provided convincing documentation that resilient youth— those who are able to survive trying and difficult events in their lives—often cite a connection with a caring adult as one factor in their success.

In the early 1990s, a scientific evaluation of Big Brothers Big Sisters (BBBS), the program perhaps most widely known for bringing adults and needy youth together, yielded persuasive evidence that supported the widespread belief of youth practitioners: mentoring worked. Young people in mentoring relationships, the research demonstrated, were less likely to use drugs and fight, more likely to attend and do better in school, and more likely to get along with peers and family members.

Complementary evidence from other programs that concentrate on the adult connection, though still limited and preliminary, is beginning to extend the findings from the BBBS study. The Quantum Opportunities Program, whose centerpiece was an extended connection between an adult counselor and poor adolescents, produced strong evidence of increasing high school completion.

Successful Mentoring Programs

The WAY (Work Appreciation for Youth) scholarship program, operated for 20 years by Children's Village in New York, has also produced strong findings. Its focus is one of the most difficult segments of the youth population—young people who have spent time in residential treatment centers (RTCs). The WAY program pairs paid adult mentor- counselors with young people for an extended period—up to five years—to ensure that the youth will have support throughout their transition to young adulthood.

Another program on the West Coast, Friends of the Children, has begun testing a similar approach with very young children who have problems sustaining social and other relationships and who are prone to being disruptive in school. The keystone of the program is a paid counselor who is committed to working with a group of these children for up to 12 years.

It should be noted that interventions of this kind are still comparatively modest in number and scale. They take their place among interventions for young people built on interaction with paid, trained professionals—teachers, social workers, foster care workers and juvenile justice staff. But they also share key elements with programs that rely heavily on adult volunteers, who supplement program activities or who—in the case of BBBS—actually constitute the core of the "intervention."

The paid mentor-counselor reflects the unique value of a "middle ground" in the youth arena: concerned and caring adults who befriend and support young people and seek to guide and mentor them, but who occupy paid positions. They are committed to staying with young people over considerable periods of time (up to 12 years). Indeed, the longevity of their connection appears to be one key to the early evidence of success that programs of this kind are producing.

FOURTEEN

Positive Family Values Are the Most Effective Gang Intervention

Heather MacDonald

Large cities such as Los Angeles, California, have been trying for many years to reduce gang activity. Traditional prevention and intervention programs are not working, argues Heather MacDonald in the following viewpoint. It is time for a new approach that focuses on the social problems that allow gangs to flourish, she contends. Young people are drawn to gangs as a substitute for the structure and authority they lack at home, MacDonald asserts. An emphasis on the importance of marriage and family would be an effective antigang strategy, and civic organizations should be called upon to replace gang culture with positive values, she maintains.

Heather MacDonald is a senior fellow at the Manhattan Institute in New York City and a contributing editor to the institute's publication *City Journal*. Her work has appeared in numerous publications, including the *Wall Street Journal*, the *New York Times*, and the *Washington Post*. She is the author of two books, *Are Cops Racist?* and *The Burden of Bad Ideas*. In 2005, MacDonald received the Bradley Prize for Outstanding Intellectual Achievement.

Heather MacDonald, "To Stop Gangs, Call the Scouts: A Long-Term Commitment to Instill Positive Social Values in Gang Communities Is Needed, Not Just Another Jobs Program or More Cops," *Los Angeles Times*, January 21, 2007. Reproduced by permission of the author.

The Los Angeles City Council recently paid $593,000 for a report on how to end the city's rising gang violence. The taxpayers didn't get their money's worth. The much-ballyhooed study, directed by civil rights attorney Connie Rice, makes a whopping 100 recommendations yet can't bring itself to mention the most important driver of gang involvement—family breakdown.

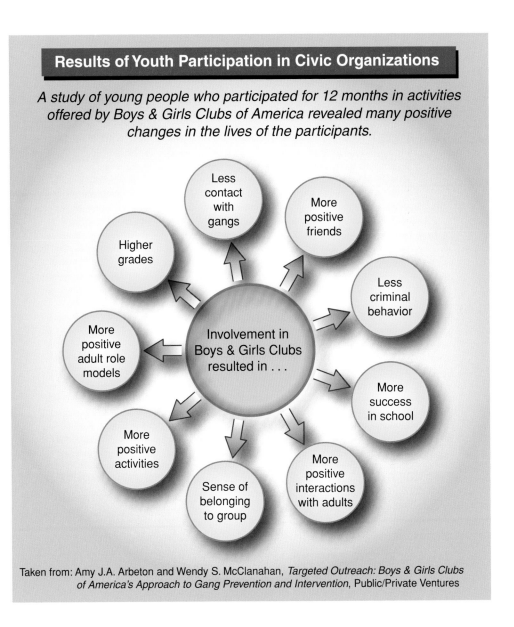

Results of Youth Participation in Civic Organizations

A study of young people who participated for 12 months in activities offered by Boys & Girls Clubs of America revealed many positive changes in the lives of the participants.

Involvement in Boys & Girls Clubs resulted in . . .

Less contact with gangs

More positive friends

Higher grades

Less criminal behavior

More positive adult role models

More success in school

More positive activities

Sense of belonging to group

More positive interactions with adults

Taken from: Amy J.A. Arbeton and Wendy S. McClanahan, *Targeted Outreach: Boys & Girls Clubs of America's Approach to Gang Prevention and Intervention*, Public/Private Ventures

"A Call to Action: A Case for a Comprehensive Solution to L.A.'s Gang Violence Epidemic" recycles all the failed nostrums from the war on poverty, such as government-created jobs, "life-skills training," "parenting education and support" and "crisis intervention." Since the 1960s, trillions of dollars have been spent on such programs without so much as making a dent in the underclass culture that gives rise to gangs. And these initiatives will never make a significant difference in that culture as long as the vast majority of young males in inner-city neighborhoods are raised without their fathers.

To be sure, plenty of heroic single mothers are bringing up law-abiding young men. But the evidence by now is overwhelming: Boys raised in fatherless homes, on average, are disproportionately likely to get involved in crime and fail in school. Without a strong paternal role model, these boys are vulnerable to the lure of macho gang culture as a surrogate for a father's authority.

The Need for Family Values

When the norm of marriage disappears from a community, further-more, the pressure for young males to become socialized evapo-rates as well. Boys in South Los Angeles and other gang-plagued neighborhoods grow up with little expectation that they will have to woo and marry the mother of their children. The standard assumption is that girls and women will raise their children by themselves, resulting in an out-of-wedlock birthrate of greater than 70%. Freed from the necessity of marriage, boys have little incentive to develop the bourgeois habits of self-discipline and deferred gratification that would make them an attractive prospect as a husband.

Compared to this overwhelming reality, Rice's jargon-ridden recommendations border on irrelevancy. For instance, Proposal 4.21, addressed to no one in particular, holds: "Acquire expert assistance to provide culturally competent, linguistically fluent, developmentally appropriate services that improve program per-formance, facilitate communication and improve access to services for immigrant and/or isolated and alienated communities."

Members of the Oriental Rascals street gang try to tackle a member of the rival Providence Street Boys gang during a football game. The game was sponsored by police in an attempt to get the gangs to settle their differences through sports, not violence.

Expanding Government Services Is Not the Answer

"A Call to Action" is also internally contradictory. Rice acknowledges that there is no evidence that the $82 million that the city already spends annually on gang interventions has had any effect. Yet she would repackage these types of programs into a huge new bureaucratic structure, which would include a deputy mayor for neighborhood safety, community action teams, a gang intervention advisory board, an expert action committee, a permanent oversight committee, an expert policy advisory board and an interagency intervention team—at an undoubtedly low-balled estimated cost of $1 billion over 18 months. If the city's social service interventions have not been working on a local scale, there is no reason to think that going large scale with them, or coordinating them better, will markedly improve their effectiveness. To her credit, Rice says that nonperforming programs should be terminated or changed. Even if such an unprecedented bureaucratic miracle occurred, her assumption that there are performing programs to fill up a new department of neighborhood safety is ungrounded.

Fortunately, the city has within its reach a proven method for reducing violence: law enforcement. The data-driven, accountable policing pioneered by Police Chief William J. Bratton is the most successful government innovation of the last decade. Getting criminals off the streets and deterring others from joining them is the surest way to bring public safety to a community, and Bratton's policing revolution has proved wildly successful in doing just that, in L.A. and elsewhere.

Identifying Appropriate Government Responses

But the Los Angeles Police Department remains preposterously understaffed. The city's top gang-fighting priority must be to bring more officers into the department so that commanders have the manpower they need to carry out Bratton's methods to their fullest extent.

Los Angeles County also must end the shameful triage in its jail system that puts criminals back on the streets before their sentences run out. It is unconscionable that the county has failed in its obligation to the public for so long.

Rice's war-on-poverty-era proposals put the cart before the horse. Effective policing is the prerequisite to her grander schemes. She wants a government job-creation program, yet no entrepreneur is going to locate in a neighborhood where criminals operate with impunity.

The understandable desire to eliminate the root causes of gang violence will remain, however, no matter how unpromising the record of government-led social uplift. The police cannot do it alone. If there is to be a bureaucratic effort to bring about social change, at least aim it at the right goal: changing the values that give rise to gang violence. An all-out campaign to restore the norm of marriage to inner-city communities, if successful, would be the most powerful antidote to gang culture. (A healthy realism must acknowledge, however, that such a goal may prove as elusive to policymakers as ending underclass poverty.)

The city should encourage philanthropic institutions that make the cultivation of positive values their core mission. A brigade of Boy Scout troops throughout Boyle Heights and Watts would do more to teach boys the importance of persistence, hard work and respect for authority than 1,000 social service and gang-intervention workers ever could. By giving youth a positive moral code, the Scouts and similar civic groups can reclaim lives and replace gang culture with true achievement.

What You Should Know About Gangs

What Is a Gang?

Gangs are usually defined as groups of people who act together to commit crimes. The type of crime may be different for each gang, although many gangs are involved with illegal guns and drugs. Gang membership and the specific activities of each gang can also vary, making it difficult to define a gang using strict criteria. Most gangs, however, have certain things in common, and police departments often use a set of characteristics to identify gangs in their communities.

In general, police departments define a gang as any group that meets five or more of these criteria:

- Has a recognized name
- Meets or hangs out together frequently
- Has recognized members who have passed an initiation
- Maintains a hierarchy or ranking among members
- Has a leader who makes and enforces rules and gives orders
- Has membership associated with a specific neighborhood, street, or other area
- Claims and defends a territory associated with a specific street, neighborhood, or other area
- Creates and maintains fear in the territory or community
- Uses special clothing, colors, tattoos, or other symbols to represent membership
- Uses special handshakes or gestures known as hand signs
- Uses special slang words and phrases
- Uses graffiti symbols on walls and personal items such as school lockers and notebooks

- Commits crimes and violent acts, often involving illegal guns and drugs

Where Are Gangs Found?
- Gangs are present in every state in the USA.
- Gangs operate in cities and towns of all sizes, including suburban and rural areas.
- Gangs exist in almost half of all the high schools in the country.
- Gangs are found in more than one third of all the middle schools in the country.
- There are an estimated twenty-five thousand different gangs in the United States.

Who Joins Gangs?
All kinds of people join gangs, but most gang members are urban teenagers and young adults. Researchers have found that certain types of teens are more likely to join a gang than others. Although it is difficult to predict with certainty who will join a gang, those who are at risk of becoming involved with a gang often meet several of the following criteria:
- Live in a neighborhood where gangs are present
- Have a parent or family member who is in a gang
- Have an unstable family life with little or no positive adult supervision
- Have few or no positive adult role models of their own ethnicity
- Feel a lack of safety in their neighborhood, school, or home
- Experience violence, crime, drug use, and/or sexual activity at a young age
- Do poorly in school and have no goals for the future
- Have friends who are involved with crime or violence
- Have friends who are in a gang
- Have few or no opportunities for positive social and recreational activities
- Have few or no opportunities to earn money legally
- Do not have the skills or education to get a legal job

- Have no opportunities to feel a sense of belonging in a positive group
- Have low self-esteem

Facts About Gang Members:
- The average gang member in the United States is seventeen to eighteen years old.
- More than half of all gang members are over the age of eighteen.
- Almost half of all gang members are under the age of eighteen.
- One fourth of all gang members are fifteen to seventeen years old.
- An estimated 94 percent of gang members are male.
- An estimated 6 percent of gang members are female.
- Almost half of all gangs have female members.
- Almost half of all gang members are Hispanic.
- Almost half of all gang members are African American.
- About one in ten gang members are white, Asian American, Native American, or other ethnicity.
- There are an estimated 750,000 gang members in the United States—about the same number of people as the whole population of a city the size of San Francisco, California; Indianapolis, Indiana; or Jacksonville, Florida.

Why Do Children and Teens Join Gangs?

People join gangs for a variety of reasons. Some common reasons for gang membership include:
- Peer pressure
- Wanting to belong to a group
- Having friends or family members in a gang
- Wanting to feel powerful and respected
- Wanting to feel safe through the protection of the gang
- Wanting the money earned through drug sales, robbery, or other crimes
- Looking for excitement

Consequences of Gang Membership

Those who are involved with gangs often believe that membership has many benefits such as money, power, protection, and safety; however, these false perceptions ignore the reality of being in a gang. Gang members face serious consequences, including:

- Being sixty times more likely to be killed than are non-members
- Being much more likely to die at a young age than are non-members
- Going to prison at a much higher rate than do nonmembers
- Developing drug and/or alcohol addictions
- Dropping out of school
- Being unable to get or hold a legal job
- Having children at a young age
- Becoming unable to have relationships with people not in the gang

What You Should Do About Gangs

Preventing Gang Involvement

One of the most effective ways of limiting the impact of gangs on a community is to prevent children and teens from ever becoming involved with a gang. Positive alternatives to gangs are often developed for adolescents and teens, but children as young as seven or eight years of age can also be recruited by gangs. The most successful gang-prevention programs are those that provide opportunities for children of all ages. Successful gang-prevention programs often include:

- Youth education about the dangers of being in a gang
- Positive social and recreational alternatives to gangs
- Opportunities for young people to make friends outside of gangs
- Assistance for young people who want to find a legal job
- Youth training in nonviolent conflict resolution
- Support for young people to resist peer pressure and build self-esteem

- Participation of community members to reduce the influence of gangs
- Partnerships between parents and teachers to reduce truancy
- Community education about gangs to help people identify the signs of gangs in the community and be aware of early gang involvement
- Former gang members who speak about the negative consequences of gang membership
- Adult role models, mentors, and tutors who work with youth at risk of gang involvement

Many organizations such as community centers, church groups, and schools provide programs to prevent young people from joining gangs. If no program exists in your community, you can explore ways to start a new program. Some ways to get involved include:

- Participating in or creating positive alternatives to gangs, such as sports, after-school programs, social clubs, or mentoring organizations
- Avoiding known gang members; hanging around them puts you at risk
- Being aware of gang colors, clothing, and symbols and avoiding them so you are not mistaken for a gang member
- Avoiding guns, knives, and other weapons, which can escalate conflicts and result in serious harm to you or others
- Joining an existing antigang group in your school or community or starting a new group with help from a teacher, church leader, or other adult
- Joining or setting up a Neighborhood Watch or community patrol with the help of the local police department
- Asking for help from school counselors or church leaders

Gang Intervention

Gang intervention programs encourage current gang members to leave the gang. The longer someone is in a gang, the harder it can be to leave, especially once initiation is done. Gang intervention is often most effective with young people who are just beginning to become involved with a gang. Community-based gang intervention programs help to identify potential gang members based on certain changes in behavior. Some of these warning signs include:

- Sudden drop in school grades or attendance
- Lack of interest in activities that were once important
- Staying out later or staying away from home more than before
- Defiance; acting aggressively or violently
- New friends who seem more aggressive
- Secretive behavior
- Change in style or color of clothing; wearing some colors exclusively or wearing clothing in a new way consistently (for example, rolling up pant legs)
- Withdrawal and lack of interest in anyone or anything outside the new group of friends
- Sudden, unexplained possession of large amounts of money or expensive items
- Use of a new nickname
- Sudden fascination with guns or other weapons
- New, unexplained cuts and bruises indicating evidence of being in a fight
- New tattoos
- Graffiti symbols on personal items such as notebooks and schoolbooks
- New or increased preference for music and movies with gang themes
- Trouble at school or with police
- Use of alcohol or drugs
- Use of hand gestures or hand signs

Getting Out of a Gang

It can be difficult to quit a gang, but it is possible. Many young people all across the country have successfully left gangs and changed their lives for the better. The National Alliance of Gang Investigators' Associations has these tips for young people who want to leave a gang:

- Never tell the gang that you plan to leave; this places you at risk.

- Find supportive adults wherever you go (school, neighborhood, recreation center) who will support you with good advice and assistance.
- Begin believing in yourself and your power to change.
- Begin spending your time doing things that are not related to the gang; look for opportunities in sports, recreation centers, Boys and Girls Clubs, arts programs, drama, school activities, and even spending time with your family.
- Try to stop looking like a gang member. For many gang members, gang clothing makes them feel safe because other people are afraid of the way they look. As you begin to believe in yourself, you will find that you don't need to make other people feel afraid in order to feel good about yourself. Stop wearing the clothes that you think have a gang meaning.
- Stop hanging out with gang members, talking like a gang member, and acting like a gang member. Find other things to say, other things to do, and other people to do them with. This is much easier if you stop dressing like a gang member first.
- Become good at making excuses. Some former gang members have said that when they started trying to leave the gang, they stopped taking phone calls from their gang friends or had their family members tell friends from the gang that they were busy or involved in some other activity.

ORGANIZATIONS TO CONTACT

The editors have compiled the following list of organizations concerned with the issues debated in this book. The descriptions are derived from materials provided by the organizations. All have publications or information available for interested readers. The list was compiled on the date of publication of the present volume; the information provided here may change. Be aware that many organizations take several weeks or longer to respond to inquiries, so allow as much time as possible.

Fight Crime: Invest in Kids
1212 New York Ave. NW, Ste. 300, Washington, DC 20005
(202) 776-0027
Web site: www.fightcrime.org

Fight Crime: Invest in Kids is a nonprofit organization with offices in ten states. Its members are law enforcement professionals and those who have been victims of violent crime. The group researches and promotes crime-prevention strategies that focus on early childhood education, prevention of child abuse and neglect, after-school programs for children and teens, and intervention programs for at-risk youth. Its Web site contains a number of research reports and other documents.

Gang Out
c/o A Better Way, Inc.
1445 Shop Rd., Columbia, SC 29201
(803) 799-0990
e-mail: abw@gangout.com
Web site: www.gangout.com

Gang Out is an educational intervention and treatment program designed to prevent or reverse gang affiliation among at-risk children and teens. It provides direct services to those in the Columbia, South Carolina, area. Its Web site includes gang prevention and intervention resources and strategies to support community-based antigang initiatives.

Gang Watchers
PO Box 2140, Porterville, CA 93258
(559) 333-4865
e-mail: info@gangwatchers.org
Web site: www.gangwatchers.org

Gang Watchers is a Christian ministry organization that works to educate and inform the public, particularly at-risk children and teens, of the dangers of gangs. It also provides assistance to churches and other organizations that want to establish similar programs. Its Web site includes extensive links to local, regional, and national news stories and Web sites related to gang crimes and gang culture. Resources are provided for those interested in getting out of a gang.

Know Gangs
621 W. Racine St., Jefferson, WI 53549
(920) 674-4493
e-mail: director@knowgangs.com
Web site: www.knowgangs.com

Know Gangs provides training and education to law enforcement agencies, social service workers, and others interested in developing programs to reduce gangs, drugs, and school violence. Its Web site offers extensive coverage of gangs and gang-related news stories, antigang services, and links to additional resources.

National Alliance of Gang Investigators' Associations (NAGIA)
PO Box 608628, Orlando, FL 32860-8694
(321) 388-8694
Web site: www.nagia.org

The National Alliance of Gang Investigators' Associations is a coalition of local, regional, and federal law enforcement agencies and other organizations focusing on gang-related issues. NAGIA's Web site includes a comprehensive library of gang-related articles on a variety of topics and profiles of many gangs currently active in the U.S.

National Center for Juvenile Justice
3700 S. Water St., Ste. 200, Pittsburgh, PA 15203
(412) 227-6950
Web site: ncjj.servehttp.com/NCJJWebsite/main.htm

The National Center for Juvenile Justice is a nonprofit resource center for information and research on topics related to any aspect of the U.S. juvenile justice system. Its Web site includes a library of research publications and statistical reports.

National Gang Center
Institute for Intergovernmental Research
PO Box 12729, Tallahassee, FL 32317
(850) 386-5356
e-mail: information@nationalgangcenter.gov
Web site: www.nationalgangcenter.gov

The National Gang Center identifies itself as a collaborative partnership between the U.S. Department of Justice, Office of Justice Programs' Bureau of Justice Assistance and the Office of Juvenile Justice and Delinquency Prevention. Recognizing that street gang activities go beyond the ages of gang members, the center promotes comprehensive antigang strategies, including prevention, intervention, suppression, investigation, and prosecution. Its Web site includes links to gang-related resources, including the National Youth Gang Center, and a library of publications, surveys, and analysis.

National Gang Crime Research Center
PO Box 990, Peotone, IL 60468-0990
(708) 258-9111
Web site: www.ngcrc.com

The National Gang Crime Research Center is an independent research organization that focuses on gang-related issues. Its Web site offers reports, profiles of active gangs, and links to additional Internet resources.

National Youth Gang Center (NYGC)
Institute for Intergovernmental Research
PO Box 12729, Tallahassee, FL 32317
(850) 385-0600
e-mail: nygc@iir.com
Web site: www.iir.com/nygc

The National Youth Gang Center is operated by the U.S. Department of Justice's Office of Juvenile Justice and Delinquency Prevention to support the reduction of youth gang involvement and gang-related crime among youth. It provides information, resources, strategies, training, and technical assistance to government agencies and antigang programs. NYGC's Web site provides access to a comprehensive collection of resources, including numerous gang-related publications, a parent's guide to gangs, and the National Youth Gang Survey report and analysis.

National Youth Violence Prevention Resource Center
PO Box 10809, Rockville, MD 20849-0809
(866) 723-3968
e-mail: NYVPRC@safeyouth.org
Web site: www.safeyouth.org

The National Youth Violence Prevention Resource Center identifies itself as a user-friendly, single point of access to U.S. federal government information on youth violence. It operates a crisis intervention hotline for youth and other victims of violence (1-866-SAFEYOUTH). Its Web site offers current information from various federal agencies for parents, youth, and other interested individuals, including a gang fact sheet covering gangs and schools, confronting the gang issue, and links to further resources.

Project Safe Neighborhoods (PSN)
e-mail: askpsn@usdoj.gov
Web site: www.psn.gov

Project Safe Neighborhoods was implemented by President George W. Bush in May 2001 as a nationwide commitment to reducing gun violence in the United States. It represents a partnership between the federal judicial system and law enforcement agencies throughout the country. PSN's Web site provides updates on various initiatives and programs, a publications archive dating back to 1997, and links to additional online resources.

FOR FURTHER RESEARCH

Books

David C. Curry, *Confronting Gangs: Crime and Community*. Los Angeles: Roxbury Park, 2002.

Tim Delaney, *American Street Gangs*. Upper Saddle River, NJ: Pearson/Prentice Hall, 2006.

Rene Denfield, *All God's Children: Inside the Dark and Violent World of Street Families*. New York: Public Affairs, 2006.

Sean Donahue, *Gangs: Stories of Life and Death from the Streets*. New York: Thunder's Mouth, 2002.

Finn-Aage Esbensen, Stephen G. Tibbetts, and Larry Gaines, eds. *American Youth Gangs at the Millennium*. Long Grove, IL: Waveland, 2004.

Tom Hayden, *Street Wars*. New York: New Press, 2005.

Charles M. Katz, *Policing Gangs in America*. New York: Cambridge University Press, 2006.

Malcolm W. Klein, *Gang Cop: The Words and Ways of Officer Paco Domingo*. Walnut Creek, CA: Altamira, 2004.

Richard C. McCorkle, *Panic: The Social Construction of the Street Gang Problem*. Upper Saddle River, NJ: Prentice Hall, 2002.

Laura Mihailoff, "Youth Gangs." In *Encyclopedia of Children and Childhood in History and Society*, ed. Paula S. Fass. New York: Macmillan Reference USA, 2004.

Antonio Nicaso, *Angels, Mobsters and Narco-Terrorists: The Rising Menace of Global Criminal Enterprises*. Hoboken, NJ: Wiley, 2005.

Randall G. Shelden, *Youth Gangs in American Society*. Belmont, CA: Thomson/Wadsworth, 2004.

James Diego Vigil, *A Rainbow of Gangs: Street Cultures in the Mega-City*. Austin: University of Texas Press, 2002.

Richard Worth, *Gangs and Crime*. Philadelphia: Chelsea House, 2002.

Periodicals

James Bell and Nicole Lim, "Young Once, Indian Forever: Youth Gangs in Indian Country," *American Indian Quarterly*, Summer/Fall 2005.

Daren Briscoe, "'Netbangers' Beware: Street Gangs Are Going Online to Compare Notes and Pick Fights. But the Cops Are Right Behind Them," *Newsweek*, March 13, 2006.

Arian Campo-Flores, "Gangland's New Face: The South Sees a Surge in Violence by Latino Groups," *Newsweek*, December 8, 2003.

————. "The Most Dangerous Gang in America: They're a Violent Force in 33 States and Counting. Inside the Battle to Police Mara Salvatrucha," *Newsweek*, March 28, 2006.

Economist, "Going Global: Gangs," February 26, 2005.

Economist, "Out of the Underworld—Criminal Gangs in the Americas," January 7, 2006.

Mark D. Freado and Sakeith Long, "I Know I Can Do It," *Reclaiming Children and Youth*, Winter 2005.

Houston Chronicle, "Ganging Up on Gangs: Politicians, Police and School Officials Urgently Need to Work Together to Combat Spiraling Youth Violence," editorial, December 17, 2006.

Liz Martinez, "Gangs in Indian Country: The Growing Phenomenon of Native American Gangs," *Law Enforcement Technology*, February 2005.

Michael Martinez, "Gang 'Capital' Steps Up Fight: Stung by Failure to Quell Problem, L.A. Goes Gung-Ho," *Chicago Tribune*, February 4, 2007.

Modesto Bee, "Concerted Effort Cut into Gang Violence," editorial, September 3, 2006.

Chitra Ragavan, Monika Guttman, and Jon Elliston, "Terror on the Streets," *U.S. News & World Report*, December 13, 2004.

Luis Rodriguez, "The End of the Line: California Gangs and the Promise of Street Peace," *Social Justice*, Fall 2005.

Katherine Rosenberg, "MySpace: A Place for Gangs; Detectives Using Web Site to Search for Gang Members," *Victorville (CA) Daily Press*, November 5, 2006.

Angela Rozas, "Cyberspace Offers New Turf for Gangs: Police Are Mining Internet Sites for Information on Local Groups Taking Their Message Online," *Chicago Tribune*, May 19, 2006.

Rupa Shenoy, "The Warriors: Hardened by Gang Life, Many Young Latinos Leaving Prison Are Now Using Their Toughness to Help Others," *Chicago Reporter*, March 2005.

Internet Sources

Lianne Archer and Andrew M. Grascia, "Girls, Gangs, and Crime—Profile of the Young Female Offender," *Social Work Today*, 2005. www.socialworktoday.com/archive/swt_0305p38.htm.

Mandalit del Barco, "The International Reach of the Mara Salvatrucha," *All Things Considered*, March 17, 2005. www.npr .org/templates/story/story.php?storyId=4539688.

Reynard Blake Jr., "Dismantling the 'Bling': Another Look at Hip-Hop," *Black Commentator*, July 15, 2004. www.blackcommenta tor.com/99/99_hip_hop.html.

Victor J. Blue, "Gangs Without Borders: Violent Central American Gangs Were Born in the USA, Returned to Their Homeland and Now Migrate Back and Forth Between Here and There," *San Francisco Chronicle*, April 2, 2006. www.sfgate.com/cgi-bin/ article.cgi?f=/c/a/2006/04/02/INGGTIOB3I1.DTL.

Clive Bradley, "Gangs, Guns and the Music of the Streets," *Solidarity 3/21*, January 11, 2003. www.workersliberty.org/node/530.

Charlie Brennan, "Gangsta Lyrics Sell a Dark Life," *Rocky Mountain News*, February 17, 2007. www.rockymountainnews.com/drmn/ other_spotlight/article/0,2777,DRMN_239605358218,00.html.

William Christenson and Sanford Newman, "Caught in the Crossfire: Arresting Gang Violence by Investing in Kids," *Fight*

Crime: Invest In Kids, 2004. www.fightcrime.org/reports/gangre port.pdf.

Rob Eshman, "Gangs of N.Y.—and L.A.," *Jewish Journal,* January 26, 2007. www.jewishjournal.com/home/preview.php?id=17140.

GirlsHealth.org, "Bullying—for Girls—Youth Gangs," December 2006. www.girlshealth.gov/bullying/youthgangs.htm.

Earl Ofari Hutchinson, "Wrong Way to Gang Bust," *AlterNet,* May 13, 2005. www.alternet.org/story/22003/.

Panama Jackson, "Reading, 'Riting, and Rap," *AllHipHop .com,* November 2005. www.allhiphop.com/editorial/index .asp?ID=283.

Samuel Logan and Ashley Morse, "The Mara Salvatrucha Organization and the U.S. Response," *PINR: Power and Interest News Report,* January 31, 2007. www.pinr.com/report .php?ac=view_report&report_id=610&language_id=1.

Heather MacDonald, "Immigration and the Alien Gang Epidemic: Problems and Solutions." Testimony before House Judiciary Committee, Subcommittee on Immigration, Border Security, and Claims, April 13, 2005. www.manhattan-institute.org/html/ mac_donald04-13-05.htm.

Alexandra Marks, "Hip-Hop Tries to Break Image of Violence," *Christian Science Monitor,* November 14, 2002. www.csmonitor .com/2002/1114/p01s04-ussc.html.

Greg Mathis, "Time to Try Another Approach to Address the Growing Gang Problem—and Not Just in L.A.," *Black America Web,* February 2, 2007. www.blackamericaweb.com/site.aspx/say itloud/mathis202.

John H. McWhorter, "How Hip-Hop Holds Blacks Back: Violence, Misogyny, and Lawlessness Are Nothing to Sing About," *City Journal,* Summer 2003. www.city-journal.org/html/13_3_how_ hip_hop.html.

Michigan State University, "Criminal Justice Resources: Gangs," November 21, 2006. www.lib.msu.edu/harris23/crimjust/gangs .htm.

National Youth Gang Center, "National Youth Gang Survey Analysis," 2006. www.iir.com/nygc/nygsa/.

Jo Seavey-Hultquist, "Keeping Girls Gang Free," Girl Scouts of the USA, 2007. www.girlscouts.org/for_adults/volunteering/articles/keeping_girls_gang_free.asp.

Pierre Thomas, Jack Date, and Nitya Venkataraman, "Preteen Gangbangers Go Digital," KTRE-TV, February 19, 2007. www.ktre.com/Global/story.asp?S=6108520&nav=2FH5.

Jon Ward, "Gang Follows Illegal Aliens," *Washington Times*, May 5, 2005. www.washtimes.com/metro/20050504-115113-3615r.htm.

PICTURE CREDITS